CW01530275

Standard Grade | General | Credit

Modern Studies

General Level 2002

Credit Level 2002

General Level 2003

Credit Level 2003

General Level 2004

Credit Level 2004

General Level 2005

Credit Level 2005

General Level 2006

Credit Level 2006

Leckie × Leckie

First exam published in 2002.
Published by Leckie & Leckie Ltd, 3rd Floor, 4 Queen Street, Edinburgh EH2 1JE
tel: 0131 220 6831 fax: 0131 225 9987 enquiries@leckieandleckie.co.uk www.leckieandleckie.co.uk

ISBN 1-84372-408-1 ISBN-13 978-1-84372-408-7

A CIP Catalogue record for this book is available from the British Library.

Printed in Scotland by Scotprint.

Leckie & Leckie is a division of Granada Learning Limited.

Leckie & Leckie is grateful to the copyright holders, as credited at the back of the book, for permission to use their material. Every effort has been made to trace the copyright holders and to obtain their permission for the use of copyright material. Leckie & Leckie will gladly receive information enabling them to rectify any error or omission in subsequent editions.

2002 | General

[BLANK PAGE]

G

2640/402

NATIONAL
QUALIFICATIONS
2002

THURSDAY, 30 MAY
10.20 AM–11.50 AM

MODERN STUDIES
STANDARD GRADE
General Level

1 Read every question carefully.

2 Answer all questions as fully as you can.

3 If you cannot do a question, go on to the next one. Try again later.

4 In question 3, answer **one** section only.

5 Write your answers in the answer book provided. Indicate clearly, in the left hand margin, the question and section of question being answered. Do not write in the right hand margin.

SCOTTISH
QUALIFICATIONS
AUTHORITY

PIB 2640/402 6/3/19570

SYLLABUS AREA 1—LIVING IN A DEMOCRACY

QUESTION 1

(*a*)

> "More *members* should ***take part*** *in trade union activities.*"

Describe **two** ways in which *members* can ***take part*** *in trade union activities.*

(Knowledge and Understanding, **4** marks)

(*b*) Study Sources 1 and 2 below, then answer the question which follows.

SOURCE 1

Women in UNISON

UNISON is an example of a Trade Union in which women are well-represented. 72% of the membership of UNISON is female, and the proportion has been increasing quickly over recent years.

The role of Trade Unions has changed over recent years. UNISON is concerned about issues such as education, child-care, racism and sexual harassment. More women are becoming involved in union activities and taking on positions as Union officials.

SOURCE 2

Women and the TGWU

The TGWU is one of the largest Unions in the country. 26% of its members are female—which is a big increase compared to a few years ago. Despite increasing numbers of female members, not many women have become Union officials.

Issues such as education, child-care, sexual harassment and racism are important for the TGWU. These used to be less important, but the work of Trade Unions has changed as time has passed.

Sources 1 and 2 give different views about the representation of women in trade unions.

Write down **two** of the differences between these views.

You must use only information from the Sources above.

(Enquiry Skills, **4** marks)

QUESTION 1 (CONTINUED)

(*c*)

People should use their ***right*** *to vote.*

Give **two** reasons why *people should use their* ***right*** *to vote.*

(Knowledge and Understanding, **4** marks)

(*d*) Study Sources 1 and 2 below, then answer the question which follows.

SOURCE 1

Typical Council Tax, 2001/2	
City of Edinburgh	£960
City of Glasgow	£1120
Scottish Borders	£785
Western Isles	£350

SOURCE 2

Extract from Radio News Broadcast

Council tax bills in Scotland increased by as much as 10% between 2000 and 2001. Council leaders have blamed the Scottish Executive for not giving them enough money to run services. However, some councils say that they will be able to increase spending on education and social work.

View of Norman Anderson

Using **only** Sources 1 and 2, give **two** reasons to support the view of Norman Anderson.

You must use only information from the Sources above.

(Enquiry Skills, **4** marks)

[Turn over

SYLLABUS AREA 2—CHANGING SOCIETY

QUESTION 2

(*a*) Study Sources 1 and 2 below, then answer the question that follows.

SOURCE 1

Regional Unemployment—1998 and 1999

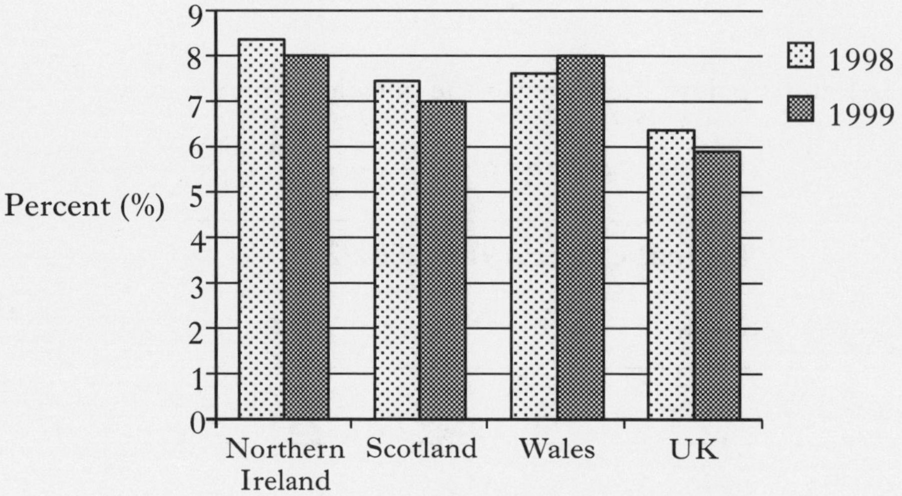

SOURCE 2

Unemployment in Selected EU Countries—1999 (%)	
France	11·0
Germany	9·1
Italy	12·0
Netherlands	3·2
Portugal	4·8
Spain	15·6
Sweden	6·8
UK	5·9
EU Average	9·3

> Scotland's unemployment rate is higher than the UK average. Unemployment in Scotland is increasing. The rate of unemployment in the UK is below the EU average. The Netherlands, Sweden and Portugal all have lower unemployment than the UK.

View of Opposition Spokesperson

Using **only** Sources 1 and 2 above, give **two** reasons why the Opposition Spokesperson could be accused of **exaggeration**.

You must use only information from the Sources above.

(Enquiry Skills, **4** marks)

QUESTION 2 (CONTINUED)

(*b*) There are many ways that *the **needs** of unemployed people* can be met by the government.

Describe **two** ways in which the government helps meet *the **needs** of unemployed people.*

(Knowledge and Understanding, **4** marks)

(*c*) *Families with young children do not all have the same standard of living.*

Give **two** reasons why *families with young children do not all have the same standard of living.*

(Knowledge and Understanding, **4** marks)

(*d*) Study the information below then answer the question which follows.

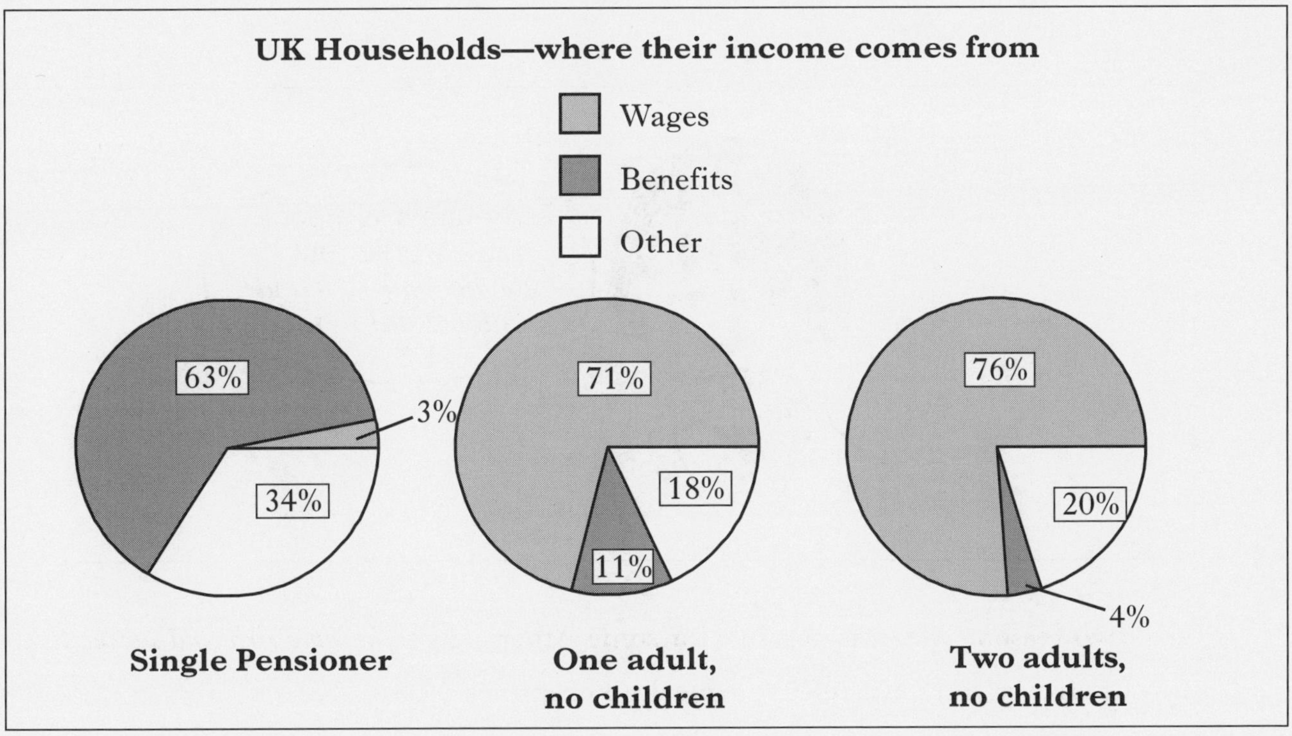

Write down **two** conclusions that can be reached about where different types of households get their income.

In your answer you should **compare different types of household**.

You must use only information from the Sources above.

(Enquiry Skills, **4** marks)

[Turn over

SYLLABUS AREA 3—IDEOLOGIES

QUESTION 3

Answer **ONE** section only: Section (A)—The USA on pages six to eight

OR Section (B)—Russia on pages nine to eleven

OR Section (C)—China on pages twelve to fourteen

(A) **THE USA**

(*a*)

Housing	Health	Crime and Justice

Choose **one** of the topics listed above.

Describe **two** ways in which some members of **ethnic minority groups** in the USA are not treated **equally** in the topic you have chosen.

In your answer you must refer to ethnic minorities in the USA that you have studied.

(Knowledge & Understanding, **4** marks)

(*b*)

Give **two** reasons why it is possible for some Americans to *become rich and successful*.

In your answer you must refer to American examples.

(Knowledge & Understanding, **4** marks)

QUESTION 3 (A) (CONTINUED)

(*c*) Study Sources 1 and 2 below, then answer the question which follows.

SOURCE 1

The USA—Presidential Election 2000			
Candidate	*Popular Votes*	*States Won**	*Electoral College Votes*
Gore (Democrat)	50·9 million	21	266
Bush (Republican)	50·4 million	30	271
Others	3·9 million	0	0

* includes Washington DC

SOURCE 2

Bush was elected President—Who did the people of the USA really want?

According to a CBS News poll, most Americans are satisfied with the outcome of the Presidential election. 55% said they were satisfied while 45% said they were not satisfied with the result.

Women of all races preferred Gore to Bush by 54% to 43%. Men, on the other hand, voted for Bush by 53% to 42%. A large majority of Black voters preferred Gore, while a small majority of White voters preferred Bush.

Most men are happy with the result of the 2000 Presidential election in the USA. The person with the most popular votes became President.

View of Eva Kaye, Florida voter

Using **only** Sources 1 and 2 above, give **one reason** to **support** and **one reason** to **oppose** the view of Eva Kaye.

You must use only information from the Sources above.

(Enquiry Skills, **4** marks)

[Turn over

QUESTION 3 (A) (CONTINUED)

(*d*) Study Sources 1 and 2 below, then answer the question which follows.

SOURCE 1

Report in an American Newspaper

The **School Voucher Program** will allow parents to use taxpayers money to send their children to private schools instead of government-run schools.

The **School Voucher Program** will take money away from government-run schools and cause them huge problems. The **School Voucher Program** will hurt the very people it is meant to help—poor ethnic minority communities. Parents of able pupils will use these vouchers to pay for private education. This will leave government-run schools with even fewer resources and funds and cause even more problems for ethnic minorities.

SOURCE 2

Government-run Schools—Statistics

	1992	*1996*	*2000*
On Internet (%)	20 (est)	65	97
Completing High School (%)			
All	79	82	84
White	83	86	89
Black	68	75	77
Hispanic	53	53	57

"The **School Voucher Program** allows parents to send their children to private schools. More pupils, of all ethnic groups, are completing High School. The School Voucher Program will benefit all pupils. Government-run schools do not have modern facilities like access to the Internet."

View of Jay Schulz

Using **only** Sources 1 and 2 above, give **two reasons** why Jay Schulz could be accused of **exaggeration**.

You must use only information from the Sources above.

(Enquiry Skills, **4** marks)

NOW GO TO QUESTION 4 ON PAGE FIFTEEN

QUESTION 3 (CONTINUED)

(B) **RUSSIA**

(*a*)

Some *national groups within Russia are not treated fairly.*

Describe **two** ways in which some members of *national groups within Russia are not treated fairly.*

In your answer you must refer to national groups in Russia that you have studied.

(Knowledge & Understanding, **4** marks)

(*b*)

The Russian Government now encourages foreign businesses to open in places such as Moscow.

Give **two** reasons why *the Russian Government now encourages foreign businesses to open in places such as Moscow.*

In your answer you must refer to specific examples.

(Knowledge & Understanding, **4** marks)

[Turn over

QUESTION 3 (B) (CONTINUED)

(*c*) Study Sources 1 and 2 below, then answer the question which follows.

SOURCE 1

Political Parties in the Duma, March 2001

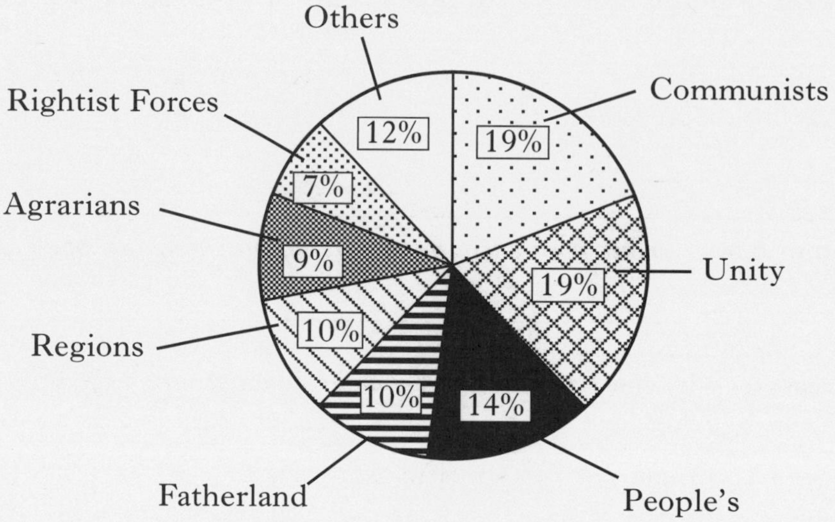

SOURCE 2

Vladimir Putin—The Man for Russia?

Vladimir Putin became President of the Russian Federation in March 2000. The previous President, Boris Yeltsin, had been in poor health for several years.

The election campaign was hard-fought, but Putin was always the favourite to win. He had been approved by Boris Yeltsin and had a spell in temporary charge of the country before the election took place. This was because Yeltsin was ill and it gave Putin the chance to prove he would be a good President. Putin gained 53% of the vote in the 2000 Presidential election, easily defeating his nearest rival Gennady Zyuganov. When the votes were counted Zyuganov had just under 30%.

One party has an overall majority in the Duma. Vladimir Putin was a clear winner in the 2000 Presidential election.

View of Yevgeny Lovchev

Using **only** Sources 1 and 2 above, give **one reason** to **support** and **one reason** to **oppose** the view of Yevgeny Lovchev.

You must use only information from the Sources above.

(Enquiry Skills, **4** marks)

QUESTION 3(B) (CONTINUED)

(*d*) Study Sources 1 and 2 below, then answer the question which follows.

SOURCE 1

Share of Total Employment in Russia, 1990 and 1998 (%): Selected Jobs		
Job Type	*1990*	*1998*
Industry	30·3	22·2
Agriculture and Fishing	13·2	13·0
Construction	12·0	8·5
Transport and Commerce	6·6	7·9
Retail	7·8	14·0
Housing	4·3	5·8

SOURCE 2

Letter to the Editor of a Russian Newspaper

Sir,

I am writing on behalf of the coal miners in the Vorkuta region of Northern Russia. The coal mines of our area produce huge amounts of coal that are vital to Russia's economy.

Due to poor management many of the miners have not been paid on a regular basis for several months now. Their families are suffering because of this situation. The government in Moscow must act now to make sure that essential workers are paid!

Yours in comradeship,

Vladimir Yuran

Jobs in industry are still the most important employment sector in Russia. The Construction industry has seen an increase in importance. All Russian workers are now paid on a regular basis. The coal miners of the Vorkuta region produce coal that is vital to the Russian economy.

View of Boris Demiananko

Using **only** Sources 1 and 2 above, give **two reasons** why Boris Demiananko could be accused of **exaggeration**.

You must use only information from the Sources above.

(Enquiry Skills, **4** marks)

NOW GO TO QUESTION 4 ON PAGE FIFTEEN

QUESTION 3 (CONTINUED)

(C) **CHINA**

(*a*)

People in some regions of China feel that they are not treated ***equally****.*

Describe **two** ways in which *people in some regions of China feel that they are not treated* ***equally****.*

In your answer you must refer to people from regions of China that you have studied.

(Knowledge and Understanding, **4** marks)

(*b*)

The Chinese government now encourages some foreign businesses to open in China.

Give **two** reasons why *the Chinese government now encourages foreign businesses to open in China.*

In your answer you must refer to specific examples.

(Knowledge and Understanding, **4** marks)

QUESTION 3(C) (CONTINUED)

(*c*) Study Sources 1 and 2 below, then answer the question which follows.

SOURCE 1

Political Parties in China

Party	**Membership**
Communist Party	57 000 000
China Democratic League	105 000
China Democratic National Construction Association	50 000
China Association for Promoting Democracy	50 000
China Revolutionary Committee of the Kuomingtang	40 000
China Peasants and Workers Democratic Party	40 000
Jisuan Society	40 000
Chinese Party for the Public Interest	10 000

SOURCE 2

Communism at the Crossroads

The Chinese Communist Party celebrated its 80th anniversary on July 1st 2001. Some members remain loyal to the teachings of Mao Ze Dong and want no change to hard-line policies. Wang Chaglin, manager of a state company, has just set up the Mao Zedong Thought website and says it receives thousands of hits every day. Other members want to see the Chinese Communist Party become more modern. The 16th Communist Party Congress, due to take place in 2002, will see new leaders introduced and policy changes proposed.

The Communist Party is the largest political party in China. All members of the party agree on future policies.

View of Fan Zhiyi

Using **only** Sources 1 and 2 above, give **one reason** to **support** and **one reason** to **oppose** the view of Fan Zhiyi.

You must use only information from the Sources above.

(Enquiry Skills, **4** marks)

QUESTION 3 (C) (CONTINUED)

(*d*) Study Sources 1 and 2 below then answer the question which follows.

SOURCE 1

April 1st

Collision between a Chinese fighter jet and an American spy plane aircraft. The Chinese pilot dies and the American crew are detained in China.

April 2nd

Investigation reveals that the Chinese jet rammed the spy plane, causing it to crash land. The Americans are denied access to the plane.

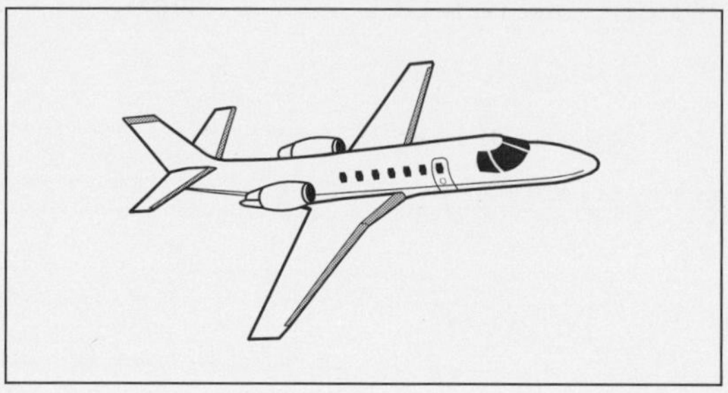

April 6th

China is not happy that the Americans will not apologise.

April 11th

The American crew are released. China still refuses to hand back the American aircraft.

SOURCE 2

Factfile

- The US military has spoken to China about five incidents in 2001 when Chinese planes came dangerously close to US flights.
- The US plane belonged to the navy and was on a routine flight above international waters.
- China is unhappy that the US is selling weapons to Taiwan.

The Chinese are correct to blame America for the incident. China is happy about American links with Taiwan.

View of Wan Zee

Using **only** Sources 1 and 2 above, give **two reasons** why Wan Zee could be accused of **exaggeration**.

You must use only information from the Sources above.

(Enquiry Skills, **4** marks)

NOW GO TO QUESTION 4 ON PAGE FIFTEEN

SYLLABUS AREA 4—INTERNATIONAL RELATIONS

QUESTION 4

(*a*) *"United Nations aid* ***meets the needs*** *of developing countries in Africa* in a number of different ways."

Describe **two** ways in which *United Nations aid* ***meets the needs*** *of developing countries in Africa*.

(Knowledge and Understanding, **4** marks)

(*b*) Study the information below, then answer the question which follows.

Selected African Countries—A comparison of levels of development in four countries

	Average Income per head ($)	*% of adults who can Read and Write*	*Life Expectancy* (Years)
Sudan	940	46	57
Ethiopia	560	35	45
Kenya	1600	78	48
Gabon	6500	63	50

Source – CIA World Factbook 2000

Compare the information about the levels of development in the four countries.

Write down **two** conclusions that can be reached about the different levels of development in the four countries.

In your answer you must **compare the countries**.

You must use only the information above.

(Enquiry Skills, **4** marks)

[Turn over for Question 4 (*c*) to (*e*) on *Page sixteen*

QUESTION 4 (CONTINUED)

You are investigating the topic in the box below.

UK aid to developing countries in Africa

Answer questions (*c*), (*d*), and (*e*) which follow.

(*c*) As part of the Planning Stage, give **two** relevant aims or headings for your investigation.

(Enquiry Skills, **2** marks)

(*d*) You have decided to write a **letter** to the Minister for Overseas Development in the UK government as a means of finding relevant information.

Give **one** advantage and **one** disadvantage of writing a letter as a way of finding out information for your investigation.

(Enquiry Skills, **4** marks)

(*e*) Give **two** relevant questions which you could include in your **letter**.

(Enquiry Skills, **2** marks)

[*END OF QUESTION PAPER*]

2002 | Credit

[BLANK PAGE]

C

2640/403

NATIONAL QUALIFICATIONS 2002

THURSDAY, 30 MAY
1.00 PM – 3.00 PM

MODERN STUDIES
STANDARD GRADE
Credit Level

1 Read every question carefully.

2 Answer all questions as fully as you can.

3 If you cannot do a question, go on to the next one. Try again later.

4 In question 3, answer **one** section only.

5 Write your answers in the answer book provided. Indicate clearly, in the left hand margin, the question and section of question being answered. Do not write in the right hand margin.

PIB 2640/403 6/3/15170

[BLANK PAGE]

SYLLABUS AREA 1—LIVING IN A DEMOCRACY

QUESTION 1

(*a*) *"MSPs **represent** their constituents in the Scottish Parliament."*

Describe, **in detail**, the ways in which *MSPs **represent** their constituents in the Scottish Parliament*.

(Knowledge & Understanding, **6** marks)

[Turn over

QUESTION 1 (CONTINUED)

(*b*) Study the information about Marchglen on *page five* opposite. Also study the information in Sources 1 and 2 below. Sources 1 and 2 contain information about the two people on the short-list to become Labour candidate for Marchglen.

Answer the question on *page five*.

SOURCE 1

Profile of Jean Alder

Jean previously worked as election agent for an unsuccessful Labour candidate. She is 55 years of age and has been a Labour Party member for 25 years.

Jean was born in London and lived there until she moved to Marchglen four years ago. Jean spent 20 years working for a major Trade Union. She earned a reputation as a tough negotiator and has experience of dealing with factory closures.

Jean's main interests apart from politics include history and gardening. She enjoys travelling and has visited Japan several times. She is married and has two grown-up children.

Extract from a campaign speech:

"I would like to see better public transport. More government money should be spent on re-training people who have lost their jobs. New skills are the key to better wage levels and living standards. We should not give help to foreign companies unless they guarantee to stay in Scotland for at least ten years—many leave when economic conditions change."

SOURCE 2

Profile of Jennifer Wood

Jennifer was born and brought up in Marchglen. Now 38 years of age, she became involved in politics 8 years ago. She has been a Local Councillor on Marchglen Council for the last four years. Two years ago she visited America and helped to attract an American computer assembly company to Marchglen, creating 400 jobs.

At the last General Election Jennifer was the election agent for a successful Labour candidate in the neighbouring constituency of Sandyknowe. Jennifer is very interested in environmental issues. She has also taken part in anti fox-hunting demonstrations.

Jennifer works as a vet but would give up her job to go into politics full-time if she became MP. She spent six years working abroad and is fluent in three foreign languages, including Japanese.

Extract from a campaign speech:

"I would like to see more encouragement for small businesses—they are the key to providing jobs in the future. We must also clean up our local environment by cutting pollution—electricity should be provided from wind-power generators. I also think that all people deserve a decent wage—too many people in Marchglen are paid low wages. I would campaign to raise the National Minimum Wage to £5 per hour."

QUESTION 1 (*b*) (CONTINUED)

Information about Marchglen constituency

- Marchglen is a constituency in Central Scotland. It is an area where traditional industries such as coal mining have closed down putting 2000 people out of work. Some new industries, including a call centre and a computer assembly plant, have been established. 80,000 people live in the constituency.
- Unemployment remains a major problem—the level is twice the average for Scotland. Wage levels in some of the new industries in Marchglen are below the national average.
- The biggest "traditional" employer is a large textile factory—but the American company which owns it has threatened to close it within the next two years. 1500 jobs could be lost.
- Environmental issues are important due to concerns about pollution from a chemical waste disposal plant in Marchglen. Local people have campaigned to have the railway to Marchglen re-opened. It was closed in the 1960s.
- At the last General Election the seat was won by Labour. However, they lost the seat to the SNP at a by-election two years ago. The SNP had a small majority of 306 at the by-election compared to a Labour majority of 5497 at the last General Election.
- The Scottish Executive and the local council have set up "Project Marchglen" to try and attract more foreign businesses to the area. A large Japanese company is considering opening a mobile phone factory in the constituency.

(*b*) (i) Using only the information about Marchglen and Sources 1 and 2 above and opposite, explain which person would be the most suitable to be selected by the Labour Party as their candidate for this constituency at the next General Election.

Give **detailed** reasons to explain your choice.

In your answer you must relate information about the candidates to the information about the constituency.

(Enquiry Skills, **6** marks)

(ii) **Explain** why you rejected the other candidate.

(Enquiry Skills, **2** marks)

[Turn over

QUESTION 1 (CONTINUED)

(*c*) Study Sources 1 and 2 below, then answer the question which follows.

SOURCE 1

Scottish Parliament (2001)—MSPs by Party and Gender			
Party	Members of the Scottish Parliament (MSPs)		
	Male	Female	Total
Labour	28	28	56
SNP	20	15	35
Conservative	15	3	18
Liberal Democrat	15	2	17
Scottish Socialist	1	0	1
Green Party	1	0	1
Independent	1	0	1
Total	**81**	**48**	**129**

SOURCE 2

UK Parliament (after 2001 General Election)—Scottish MPs by Party and Gender			
Party	Members of Parliament (MPs)		
	Male	Female	Total
Labour	45	11	56
Conservative	1	0	1
Liberal Democrat	10	0	10
SNP	4	1	5
Total	**60**	**12**	**72**

> "Women are well represented amongst Scotland's MPs and MSPs. This is true for all parties."

View of Jane Smith

Using Sources 1 and 2 above, explain why Jane Smith could be accused of being **selective in her use of facts**.

Use only information from Sources 1 and 2 in your answer.

(Enquiry Skills, **4** marks)

SYLLABUS AREA 2—CHANGING SOCIETY

QUESTION 2

(*a*) | *Some elderly people have greater health* ***needs*** *than other elderly people.* |

Explain, **in detail**, why *some elderly people have greater health* ***needs*** *than other elderly people.*

(Knowledge and Understanding, **6** marks)

(*b*) | *Some people believe that the government should increase the level of the old age pension.* |

Explain, **in detail**, why *some people believe that the government should increase the level of the old age pension.*

(Knowledge and Understanding, **4** marks)

[Turn over

QUESTION 2 (CONTINUED)

(*c*) Study Sources 1 and 2 below and opposite, then answer the question which follows.

SOURCE 1

Statistical Information—Accommodation for Elderly People in Scotland (1990 – 1999)

	1990	**1995**	**1999**
Special Needs Housing (Number of dwellings)			
Very Sheltered Housing	n/a	671	1,620
Sheltered Housing	26,737	33,687	36,708
Adapted Housing	10,456	19,013	20,216
(Total)	(37,193)	(53,371)	(58,544)
Residential Care Homes (Number of places)			
Local Authority	8,807	7,584	6,059
Private	3,195	3,934	4,477
Voluntary	4,335	3,807	3,684
(Total)	(16,337)	(15,325)	(14,220)
Private Nursing Homes (Number of places)	12,866	15,986	20,188
NHS Hospital Beds in Scotland			
Geriatric Long-stay (Residential)	9,277	7,729	4,924
Geriatric Short-stay (Assessment)	2,521	3,245	3,634
(Total)	(11,798)	(10,974)	(8,558)

Source – *Scottish Community Care Statistics, 1999*

QUESTION 2 (*c*) (CONTINUED)

SOURCE 2

Accommodation Rates for Selected Scottish Local Authorities
(all rates per thousand elderly people)

Western Isles	
Residential Care Homes	31
Special Needs Housing	43
Private Nursing Homes	12

Aberdeen City	
Residential Care Homes	19
Special Needs Housing	134
Private Nursing Homes	26

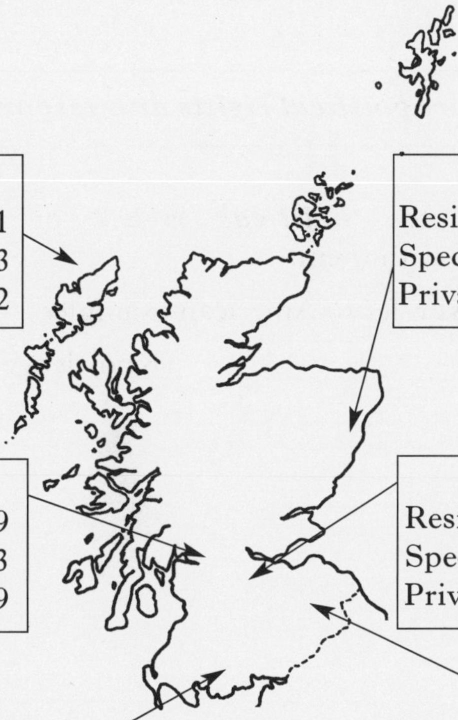

Glasgow City	
Residential Care Homes	19
Special Needs Housing	203
Private Nursing Homes	29

West Lothian	
Residential Care Homes	15
Special Needs Housing	122
Private Nursing Homes	30

Dumfries and Galloway	
Residential Care Homes	22
Special Needs Housing	57
Private Nursing Homes	16

Scottish Borders	
Residential Care Homes	18
Special Needs Housing	122
Private Nursing Homes	26

Using only the information in Sources 1 and 2 above and opposite, what **conclusions** can be reached about **accommodation for elderly people** in Scotland?

You must use information from **all** the sources.

You should reach conclusions about the following.

- Accommodation rates in different parts of Scotland
- Ways in which accommodation for elderly people has changed since 1990
- Number **and** use of NHS hospital beds
- Relationship between NHS hospital beds and other types of accommodation

(Enquiry Skills, **8** marks)

[Turn over

SYLLABUS AREA 3—IDEOLOGIES

QUESTION 3

Answer **ONE** Section only: Section (A)—The USA on pages *ten* and *eleven*.

OR Section (B)—Russia on pages *twelve* and *thirteen*.

OR Section (C)—China on pages *fourteen* and *fifteen*.

(A) **THE USA**

(*a*) *The American people have* ***political rights and responsibilities.***

Describe, **in detail**, the ***political rights*** of *American people* ***and*** the ***responsibilities*** that go with them.

In your answer you **must** refer to American examples.

(Knowledge and Understanding, **8** marks)

QUESTION 3(A) (CONTINUED)

You have been asked to carry out an investigation on the topic below.

Equality in the USA

Now answer questions (*b*), (*c*), (*d*), (*e*) and (*f*).

(*b*) State a relevant **hypothesis** for your investigation.

(Enquiry Skills, **2** marks)

(*c*) Give **two aims or headings** to help you prove or disprove your hypothesis.

(Enquiry Skills, **2** marks)

You decide to use a variety of sources to help with your investigation into this topic.

(*d*) Describe how you would find relevant **web sites** to help with your investigation.

(Enquiry Skills, **2** marks)

(*e*) Explain why using **e-mail** would be a good method of enquiry for this topic.

(Enquiry Skills, **2** marks)

(*f*) To help you carry out your investigation, your teacher gives you a **collection of Encyclopedias on 4 CD-ROMs**.

What **problems** might you have in using the information in the **collection of Encyclopedias on 4 CD-ROMs**?

(Enquiry Skills, **2** marks)

NOW GO TO QUESTION 4 ON PAGE SEVENTEEN

QUESTION 3 (CONTINUED)

(B) **RUSSIA**

(*a*) *Since the break-up of the Soviet Union, Russians have enjoyed more* ***political rights and responsibilities.***

Describe, **in detail**, the ***political rights and responsibilities*** now *enjoyed* by *Russians*.

In your answer you **must** refer to Russian examples.

(Knowledge and Understanding, **8** marks)

QUESTION 3(B) (CONTINUED)

You have been asked to carry out an investigation on the topic below.

Equality in Russia

Now answer questions (*b*), (*c*), (*d*), (*e*) and (*f*).

(*b*) State a relevant **hypothesis** for your investigation.

(Enquiry Skills, **2** marks)

(*c*) Give **two aims or headings** to help you prove or disprove your hypothesis.

(Enquiry Skills, **2** marks)

You decide to use a variety of sources to help with your investigation into this topic.

(*d*) Describe how you would find relevant **web sites** to help with your investigation.

(Enquiry Skills, **2** marks)

(*e*) Explain why using **e-mail** would be a good method of enquiry for this topic.

(Enquiry Skills, **2** marks)

(*f*) To help you carry out your investigation, your teacher gives you a **collection of Encyclopedias on 4 CD-ROMs**.

What **problems** might you have in using the information in the **collection of Encyclopedias on 4 CD-ROMs**?

(Enquiry Skill, **2** marks)

NOW GO TO QUESTION 4 ON PAGE SEVENTEEN

QUESTION 3 (CONTINUED)

(C) **CHINA**

(*a*) *Many Chinese people want more* ***political rights****.*

Describe, **in detail**, the arguments used by *Chinese people* who *want more* ***political rights****.*

In your answer you **must** refer to Chinese examples.

(Knowledge and Understanding, **8** marks)

QUESTION 3 (*c*) (CONTINUED)

You have been asked to carry out an investigation on the topic below.

Equality in China

Now answer questions (*b*), (*c*), (*d*), (*e*) and (*f*).

(*b*) State a relevant **hypothesis** for your investigation.

(Enquiry Skills, **2** marks)

(*c*) Give **two aims or headings** to help you prove or disprove your hypothesis.

(Enquiry Skills, **2** marks)

You decide to use a variety of sources to help with your investigation into this topic.

(*d*) Describe how you would find relevant **web sites** to help with your investigation.

(Enquiry Skills, **2** marks)

(*e*) Explain why using **e-mail** would be a good method of enquiry for this topic.

(Enquiry Skills, **2** marks)

(*f*) To help you carry out your investigation, your teacher gives you a **collection of Encyclopedias on 4 CD-ROMs**.

What **problems** might you have in using the information in the **collection of Encyclopedias on 4 CD-ROMs**?

(Enquiry Skills, **2** marks)

NOW GO TO QUESTION 4 ON PAGE SEVENTEEN

[BLANK PAGE]

SYLLABUS AREA 4—INTERNATIONAL RELATIONS

QUESTION 4

(*a*)

*The United Nations has used its **power** to intervene in recent conflicts in Europe.*

Choose **one** recent conflict in Europe that you have studied.

Describe, **in detail**, the role of the *United Nations* during the conflict you have chosen.

(Knowledge and Understanding, **4** marks)

(*b*)

*Some countries in Eastern Europe feel that their **needs** would be met through joining NATO.*

Explain, **in detail**, why *some countries in Eastern Europe feel that their **needs** would be met through joining NATO.*

(Knowledge and Understanding, **4** marks)

[Turn over

QUESTION 4 (CONTINUED)

(*c*) Study Sources 1, 2, 3 and 4 below and opposite, then answer the question which follows.

SOURCE 1

Britain must join the Euro

Why are the British people so hesitant and negative about the Single European Currency (Euro)? Is it because they are too narrow-minded? Do they have a fear of things foreign? Do they just love the pound? Whatever it is, it isn't based on real facts. The media refuses to highlight all the positives that will come from joining. It will protect jobs and keep prices steady throughout the EU. There is no reason to believe that the British people will lose their national identity—the UK will remain an independent country in Europe.

Sometimes British people find it hard to get excited about Europe. The fact is that Britain needs Europe and our partners in the European Union. More than 70% of UK exports go to European Union countries. This is what British prosperity has been built upon. Surely we want this to continue? The only way for this to happen is to join the Single European Currency and enjoy the benefits which it will bring.

Statement by Pro European Businessman

SOURCE 2

Eurobarometer Opinion Poll

Please state whether you Agree or Disagree with the following statement:

There has to be one single currency, the Euro, replacing the National Currencies of the member states of the European Union.

	Agree		*Disagree*		*Don't know*	
	1999	2000	1999	2000	1999	2000
*Germany	55	50	36	39	9	10
*Spain	72	75	18	18	10	7
*France	64	67	32	29	4	4
*Ireland	78	63	13	22	9	15
*Finland	47	49	49	48	4	3
UK	25	22	59	61	16	17

*Members of the Single European Currency, 2001.

SOURCE 3

What Europeans think joining the Euro will mean for them (%)

	Yes	**No**	**Don't know**
• Create more jobs	42	36	22
• Cause countries to lose too much of their national identity	25	49	26
• Make it easier for people to travel	52	32	16
• Reduce differences between the rich and not quite so rich countries of the EU	22	53	25
• Increase crime levels due to increase in fake notes and coins	61	24	15
• Lead to rising bank charges	76	18	6

QUESTION 4 (*c*) (CONTINUED)

SOURCE 4

We love the pound

The British economy is booming. Unemployment is at a record low and Britain is the envy of the rest of Europe. Why would we want to throw this away by joining the Euro? The pound is stable and inflation is low. Figures show that the value of the Euro has gone down. This worries me. It would cost billions of pounds for all British businesses to change their systems to the Euro and only a small proportion would benefit from the reduced costs of trade with Europe. Why would we want to give it up? The EU has already taken away many of the powers that we had. Do we really want Brussels to set our Interest and Tax Rates? If we join the Euro, then we will have taken a massive step down the road to giving up our national identity. This is unthinkable for the British people.

(View of Businessman opposed to EURO membership.)

Value of the Euro against the pound

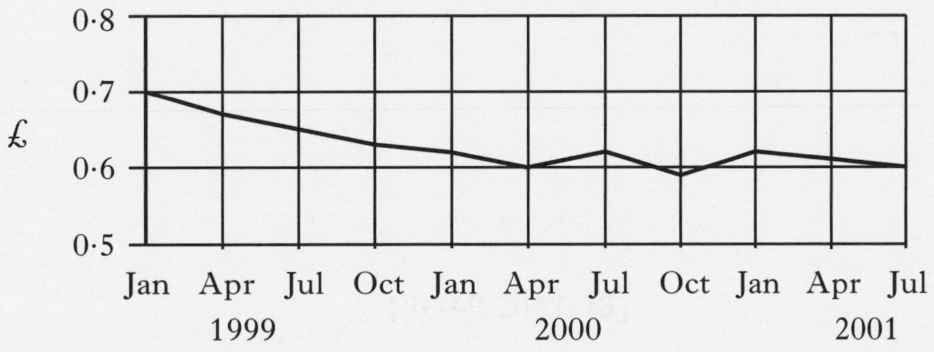

The United Kingdom should join the Single European Currency (Euro).

Using only the information from Sources 1, 2, 3 and 4 above and opposite, give arguments **for** and **against** the proposal that *the United Kingdom should join the Single European Currency (Euro).*

You should only use information from the Sources in your answer.

(Enquiry Skills, **8** marks)

(*d*) Overall, do you support the proposal? **Explain** why you have reached this decision.

(Enquiry Skills, **2** marks)

[*END OF QUESTION PAPER*]

[BLANK PAGE]

2003 | General

[BLANK PAGE]

G

2640/402

NATIONAL QUALIFICATIONS 2003

WEDNESDAY, 28 MAY
10.20 AM–11.50 AM

MODERN STUDIES STANDARD GRADE
General Level

1 Read every question carefully.

2 Answer all questions as fully as you can.

3 If you cannot do a question, go on to the next one. Try again later.

4 In question 3, answer **one** section only; Section (A) The USA or Section (B) Russia or Section (C) China.

5 Write your answers in the answer book provided. Indicate clearly, in the left hand margin, the question and section of question being answered. Do not write in the right hand margin.

THB 2640/402 6/19570

SYLLABUS AREA 1—LIVING IN A DEMOCRACY

QUESTION 1

(*a*) *"Members of the Scottish Parliament (MSPs) can **represent** their constituents* in a number of ways."

Describe **two** ways in which MSPs *can **represent** their constituents.*

(Knowledge and Understanding, **4** marks)

(*b*) Study Sources 1 and 2 below, then answer the question which follows.

SOURCE 1

GREENPEACE

Greenpeace is a powerful pressure group.

Some of Greenpeace's income comes in the form of donations from supporters. Total income for Greenpeace is about £6 million per year.

Greenpeace tries to use peaceful and legal methods of protest. However, on occasions some members have felt the need to break the law to draw attention to important issues. Greenpeace also lobbies MPs to try and change government policy.

SOURCE 2

Shelter

Shelter Scotland only uses peaceful campaign methods. Its members would never break the law to get things changed. They lobby MPs and use other legal methods.

Some of Shelter Scotland's income comes from donations from supporters and some from government grants. The total income of the organisation is about £2 million per year.

Shelter Scotland is an important Pressure Group.

"All pressure groups are the same."

View of Gina Curtis

Using Sources 1 and 2 above, give **two** reasons why Gina Curtis could be accused of **exaggeration**.

Your answer must be based entirely on the sources above.

(Enquiry Skills, **4** marks)

QUESTION 1 (CONTINUED)

You are investigating the topic in the box below.

Voting in the UK

Answer questions (*c*), (*d*), and (*e*) which follow.

(*c*) As part of the Planning Stage, give **two** relevant **aims or headings** for your investigation.

(Enquiry Skills, **2** marks)

(*d*) You have decided to carry out a **survey of public opinion** about voting in the UK.

Give **two** relevant **questions** which you could include in your survey that would help you with this investigation.

Each question should be linked to the aims or headings you used in your answer to question (*c*). Do not simply repeat the aims/headings—you should expand upon them.

(Enquiry Skills, **2** marks)

(*e*) Give **one** advantage and **one** disadvantage of using a survey of public opinion as part of an investigation.

(Enquiry Skills, **4** marks)

[Turn over

SYLLABUS AREA 2—CHANGING SOCIETY

QUESTION 2

(*a*)

> *The **needs** of some elderly people can be met by their family.*

Describe **two** ways in which *the **needs** of some elderly people can be met by their family.*

(Knowledge and Understanding, **4** marks)

(*b*)

> *Some lone parents find it more difficult to get a suitable job than other people.*

Give **two** reasons why *some lone parents find it more difficult to get a suitable job than other people.*

(Knowledge and Understanding, **4** marks)

(*c*) Study the information below, then answer the question which follows.

Help For Older People in Scotland, 1995–2000		
	1995	*2000*
Number of older people with a home help	93 471	74 058
Day care centre places	8336	7670
Sheltered housing places	34 358	36 708
Residential care home places	16 988	16 300
Nursing home places	16 674	18 498
Long stay hospital beds	7729	4924

Write down **two conclusions** that can be reached about the **changes** in the ways older people in Scotland received help between 1995 and 2000.

You must only use the information above.

(Enquiry Skills, **4** marks)

QUESTION 2 (CONTINUED)

(*d*) Study Sources 1 and 2 below, then answer the question which follows.

SOURCE 1

Newspaper Report—Scottish Daily News

Recent Government figures have shown that the average weekly income in Scotland has risen to £336. There are great differences between households. Couples with children bring home an average of £410 each week, compared to £325 for a couple without children and £155 for a single pensioner.

SOURCE 2

Percentage of Households with a Car (Scotland 2000)	
Single Adult	45%
Adult Couple—no children	80%
Adult Couple—1 child	87%
Adult Couple—2 children	83%
Lone Parent	33%

"Couples with children have a lower standard of living than other types of household."

View of Jim Douglas

Give **two reasons to oppose** the view of Jim Douglas.

You must give **one** reason from Source 1 and **one** reason from Source 2.

(Enquiry Skills, **4** marks)

[Turn over

SYLLABUS AREA 3—IDEOLOGIES

QUESTION 3

Answer **ONE** section only: Section (A)—The USA on pages six to seven

OR Section (B)—Russia on pages eight to nine

OR Section (C)—China on pages ten to eleven

(A) **THE USA**

(*a*) *The economy of the USA allows some American people to have high living standards.*

Describe **two** ways in which *the economy of the USA allows some American people to have high living standards.*

In your answer you **must** use American examples.

(Knowledge & Understanding, **4** marks)

(*b*) Study the information below, then answer the question which follows.

Income for Various Ethnic Groups in the USA (Dollars)			
	1996	*1998*	*2000*
White	20 986	22 575	23 415
Black	13 007	13 672	15 197
Hispanic	10 984	12 065	12 306

Statements made in a speech by Al Hood

- The income of all ethnic groups has been increasing in the USA.
- Blacks continue to have the lowest incomes in the USA.
- Hispanics' incomes increased more than those of blacks between 1998 and 2000.
- Whites continue to have the highest incomes of all groups.

Using **only** the information above, write down **two** statements made by Al Hood that are **exaggerated**.

Using the statistics in the table, give **one** reason why **each** of the statements you have chosen is **exaggerated**.

(Enquiry Skills, **4** marks)

QUESTION 3 (A) (CONTINUED)

(*c*) *American people should* ***participate*** *in politics.*

Give **two** reasons why *American people should* ***participate*** *in politics.*

In your answer you **must** use American examples.

(Knowledge & Understanding, **4** marks)

(*d*) Study the information below, then answer the question which follows.

Minimum age for Basic Rights in Selected American States

Minimum age for learning to drive | **Minimum age for gun ownership**

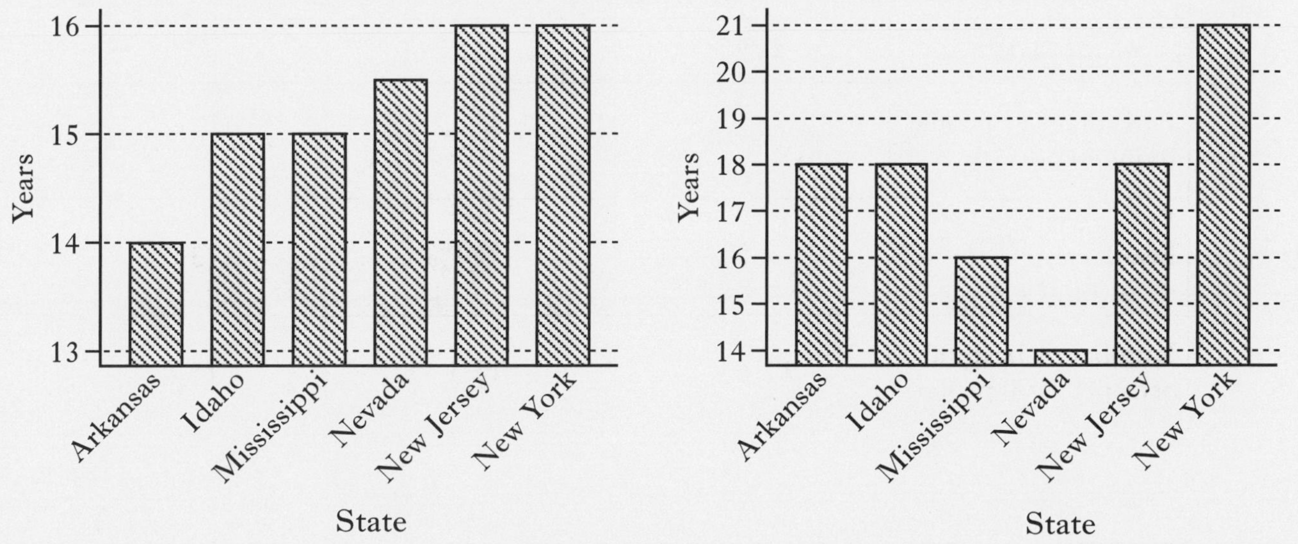

The graphs show statistics about the minimum age for basic rights in selected American states.

Write down **two conclusions** that can be reached about basic rights in selected American states.

You should write **one** conclusion about **each** of:

- the minimum age for learning to drive;
- the minimum age for gun ownership.

Your conclusions should be based entirely on the information above.

(Enquiry Skills, **4** marks)

NOW GO TO QUESTION 4 ON PAGE TWELVE

QUESTION 3 (CONTINUED)

(B) **RUSSIA**

(*a*) *Recent economic changes have led to higher living standards for some Russians.*

Describe **two** ways in which *recent economic changes have led to higher living standards for some Russians.*

In your answer you **must** use Russian examples.

(Knowledge & Understanding, **4** marks)

(*b*) Study the information below, then answer the question which follows.

Social Statistics—Russia

Social indicators	*1995*	*1997*	*1999*
Percentage of people living in poverty	26·2%	21·2%	26·2%
Public spending on health care (% of GDP)	2·9%	3·4%	3·0%
Number of hospital beds per 1000 people	12·6	12·1	11·8

Source: OECD

Statements Made in a Speech by Olga Volkova

- The percentage of people living in poverty in Russia was the same in 1999 as in 1995.
- Public spending on health care has gone down since 1995.
- The number of hospital beds per 1000 people has fallen each year since 1995.
- Between 1997 and 1999 the percentage of people living in poverty has gone down.

Using only the information above, write down **two** statements made by Olga Volkova which are **exaggerated**.

Using the statistics in the table, give one **reason** why each of the statements you have chosen is **exaggerated**.

(Enquiry Skills, **4** marks)

QUESTION 3 (B) (CONTINUED)

(*c*)	*Russian people should* ***participate*** *in politics.*

Give **two** reasons why *Russian people should* ***participate*** *in politics.*

In your answer you **must** use Russian examples.

(Knowledge & Understanding, **4** marks)

(*d*) Study the information below, then answer the question which follows.

Crime Statistics—Moscow

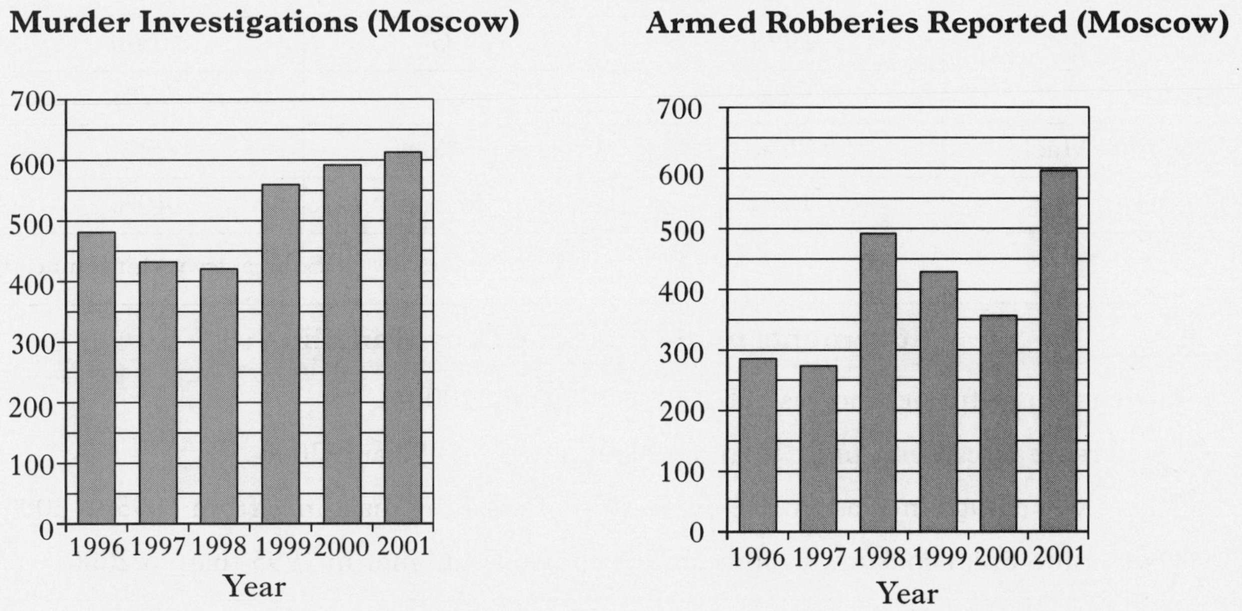

The information above shows statistics about Crime in Moscow.

Write down **two conclusions** that can be reached about changes in crime in Moscow.

You should write **one** conclusion about **each** of:

- murder investigations in Moscow;
- armed robberies reported in Moscow.

Your conclusions should be based entirely on the information above.

(Enquiry Skills, **4** marks)

NOW GO TO QUESTION 4 ON PAGE TWELVE

QUESTION 3 (CONTINUED)

(C) **CHINA**

(*a*) *Recent economic changes have led to higher living standards for some Chinese people.*

Describe **two** ways in which *recent economic changes have led to higher living standards for some Chinese people*.

In your answer you **must** use Chinese examples.

(Knowledge and Understanding, **4** marks)

(*b*) Study the information below, then answer the question which follows.

Ownership of Selected Consumer Goods—Urban Households			
	1990	*1995*	*2000*
Fridge	42%	66%	77%
Washing Machine	78%	89%	92%
Camera	19%	33%	40%

Source: www.chinaguide.org

Statements made in a speech by Han Zhu

- Ownership of fridges increased between 1990 and 2000.
- Ownership of cameras more than doubled between 1990 and 2000.
- There was a huge increase in the ownership of washing machines from 1995 to 2000.
- Ownership of all consumer goods shown above was higher in 1995 than in 2000.

Using **only** the information above, write down **two** statements made by Han Zhu which are **exaggerated**.

Using the statistics in the table, give one **reason** why **each** of the statements you have chosen is **exaggerated**.

(Enquiry Skills, **4** marks)

(*c*) *Many Chinese people cannot* ***participate*** *in politics as much as they would like.*

Give **two** reasons why *many Chinese people cannot* ***participate*** *in politics as much as they would like.*

In your answer you **must** use Chinese examples.

(Knowledge and Understanding, **4** marks)

QUESTION 3 (C) (CONTINUED)

(*d*) Study the information below, then answer the question which follows.

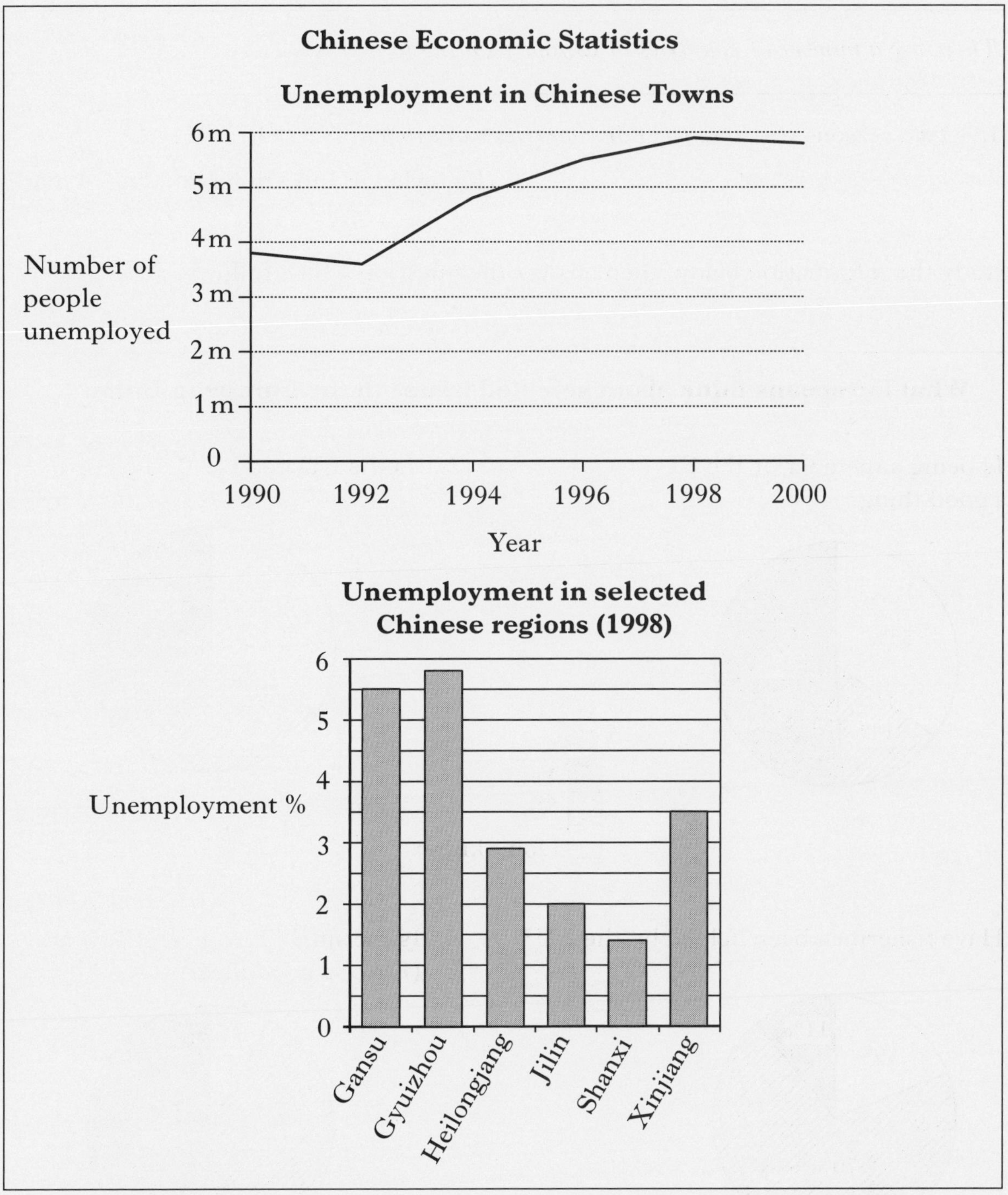

The information above shows statistics about Unemployment in China.

Write down **two conclusions** that can be reached about unemployment in China.

You should write **one** conclusion about **each** of:

- unemployment in Chinese towns since 1990;
- unemployment in selected Chinese regions.

Your conclusions should be based entirely on the information above.

(Enquiry Skills, 4 marks)

NOW GO TO QUESTION 4 ON PAGE TWELVE

SYLLABUS AREA 4—INTERNATIONAL RELATIONS

QUESTION 4

(*a*)

> *There are a number of countries in Europe wanting to join NATO.*

Give **two** reasons why *a number of countries want to join NATO.*

(Knowledge and Understanding, **4** marks)

(*b*) Study the information below, then answer the question which follows.

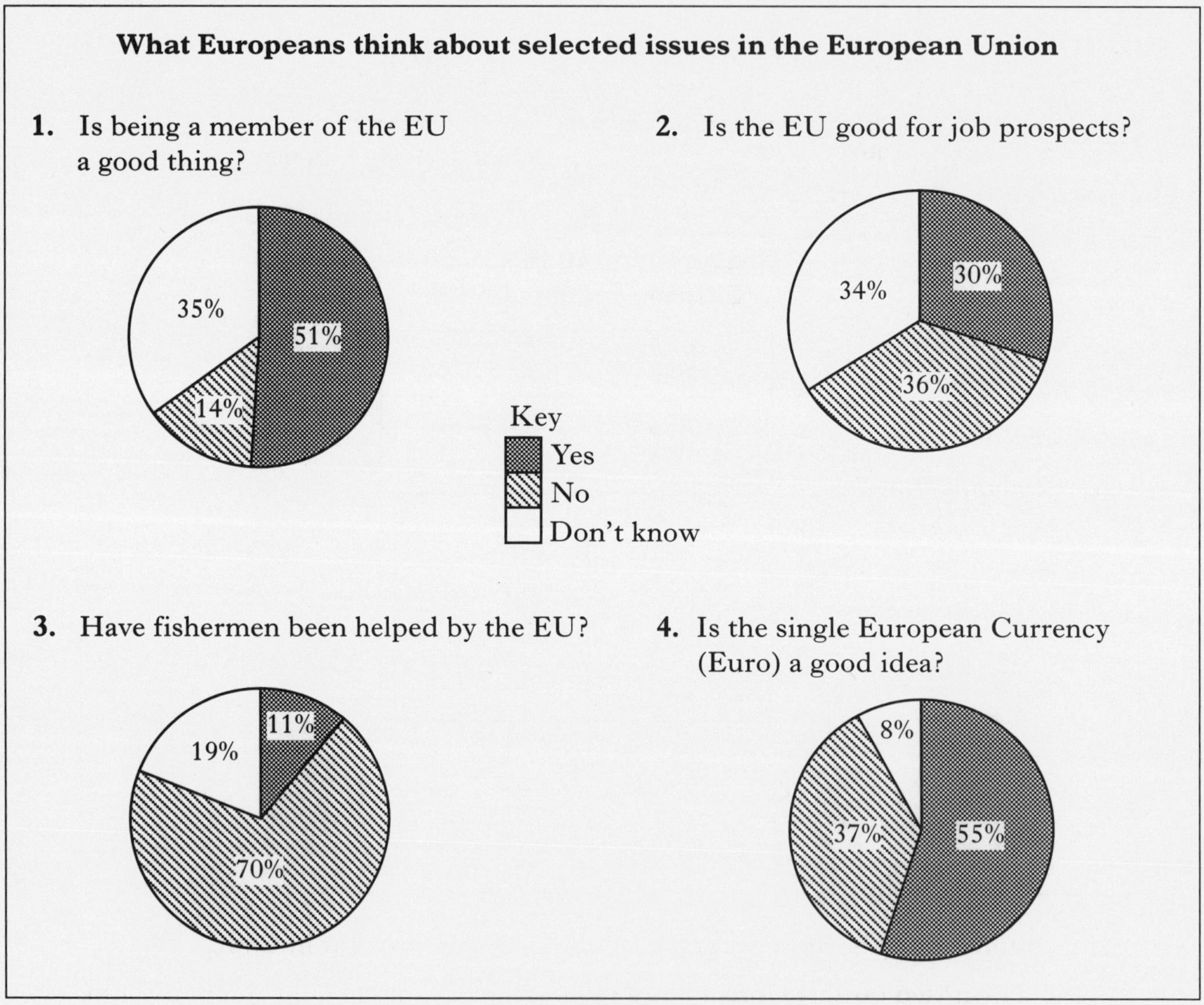

> "Most people asked are pleased with the European Union."

View of Fritz Seliger

Do you **agree or disagree** with the view of Fritz Seliger?

Give **two** reasons for your answer, based entirely on the information above.

(Enquiry skills, **4** marks)

QUESTION 4 (CONTINUED)

(*c*)

The United Nations has been involved in European conflicts.

Choose **one** European conflict which you have studied.

Describe **two** ways that *the United Nations has been involved* in the conflict.

(Knowledge and Understanding, **4** marks)

(*d*) Study Sources 1 and 2 below, then answer the question which follows.

SOURCE 1

Factfile on European Involvement in the War Against Terrorism—June 2002

- The International Red Cross offers medical and humanitarian aid.
- Germany offers 3900 troops to the coalition against terrorism.
- France sends aid to Afghanistan to help many starving people.
- Netherlands offers troops, ships and fighter planes to combat terrorism.

SOURCE 2

Opinion Poll

Question: Should your country join in military action against terrorism?

Country	Yes	No	Don't Know
United Kingdom	79	12	9
Spain	58	38	4
Germany	53	42	5

The Economist, 22/09/01

"European governments are unwilling to take military action against terrorism. In some countries a majority of people do not want military action against terrorism."

View of Bill Bridges

Using only Sources 1 and 2, give **two** reasons to **oppose** the view of Bill Bridges.

(Enquiry Skills, **4** marks)

[*END OF QUESTION PAPER*]

[BLANK PAGE]

[BLANK PAGE]

C

2640/403

NATIONAL QUALIFICATIONS 2003

WEDNESDAY, 28 MAY
1.00 PM – 3.00 PM

MODERN STUDIES
STANDARD GRADE
Credit Level

1 Read every question carefully.

2 Answer all questions as fully as you can.

3 If you cannot do a question, go on to the next one. Try again later.

4 In question 3, answer **one** section only: Section (A) The USA **or** Section (B) Russia **or** Section (C) China.

5 Write your answers in the answer book provided. Indicate clearly, in the left hand margin, the question and section of question being answered. Do not write in the right hand margin.

SCOTTISH QUALIFICATIONS AUTHORITY

THB 2640/403 6/15070

SYLLABUS AREA 1—LIVING IN A DEMOCRACY

QUESTION 1

(*a*) *Women and ethnic minorities are under-represented in the House of Commons.*

Choose **either** women **or** ethnic minorities.

Explain, **in detail**, why the group you have chosen is ***under-represented*** *in the House of Commons.*

(Knowledge & Understanding, **4** marks)

(*b*) *Trade union members have rights and responsibilities during a dispute with their employers.*

Describe, **in detail**, the **rights and responsibilities** trade union members have during a dispute with their employers.

(Knowledge & Understanding, **6** marks)

(*c*) Study Sources 1, 2 and 3 below and opposite, then answer the question which follows.

SOURCE 1

SHIRETON NEWS — NEW HOUSING CAUSES ANGER

A recent public meeting in Glenblyth village hall was attended by thirty local people. They were told about plans for 200 new houses to be built by the Booth Building Company. A company spokesperson explained that as the village was only 20 miles from a major city, there was a huge demand for housing from people employed in banking and other professional jobs. These people wished to take advantage of a beautiful rural setting with excellent schools. The chairperson of Glenblyth Action Group pointed out that expensive houses will be bought by commuters who will play no part in the life of the village. He said, "The existing village has 250 houses and most people feel that the building project would change the character of the village. It will bring no benefits to existing residents who enjoy the peace of the countryside and have a strong village community spirit."

Jim Marshall, speaking for the builders, announced that the company planned to build some expensive houses for those who could afford them, but also cheaper houses that young families who want to remain in the village could afford to buy. However, although cheaper housing was welcomed by the village, many local people put forward the view that building would add to congestion on the main road running through the village. One woman said, "Parking is a problem and there are concerns about whether fire engines and other essential services would get through."

QUESTION 1 (*c*) (CONTINUED

SOURCE 2

Opinion Poll of People in Glenblyth and surrounding area

	YES	NO	DON'T KNOW
1. Are you in favour of building 200 new houses?	21%	69%	10%
2. Do you think building 200 houses would put pressure on local facilities?	35%	33%	32%

3. Have you taken any of the following actions to protest against the building of 200 houses?

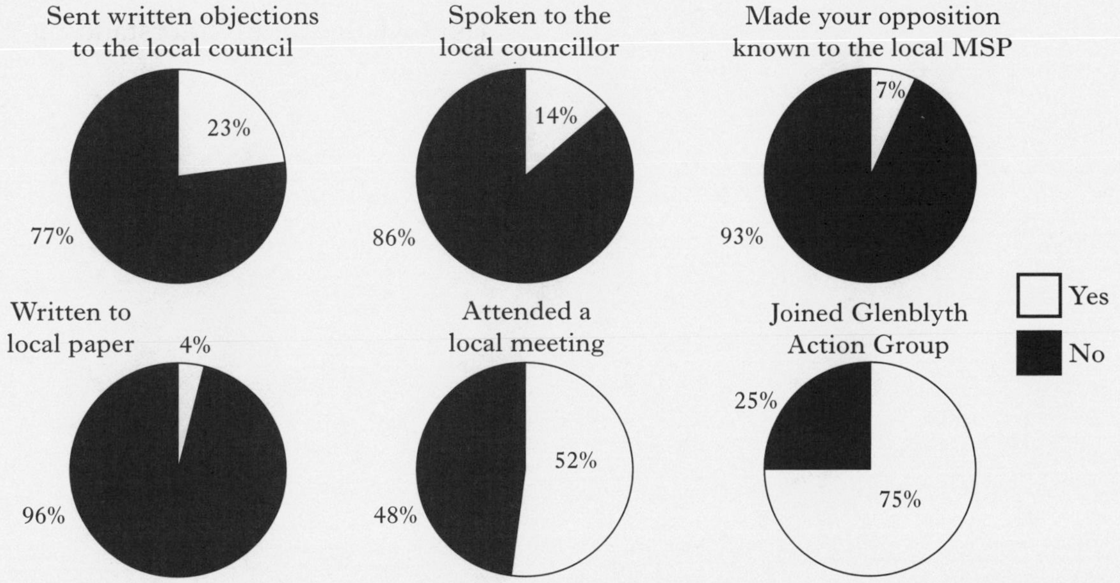

SOURCE 3

Radio Report — Live from Council Meeting

"Today, Councillors met to decide if the Booth Building Company should be given planning permission to build 200 houses in Glenblyth village. Before the meeting, a small group of 20 banner-waving protestors shouted at the Councillors as they entered Council Headquarters. The council leader later came out to address the protesters and assured them that their views would be taken into account.

After a debate, the Councillors decided to grant planning permission on condition that the builders provide at least 30 houses at the cheaper end of the market. This is John Kennedy reporting for Radio News . . . "

"People living in Glenblyth support the plan to build 200 new houses."

View of John Cornwall, Chairman of Booth Building Company

Using only Sources 1, 2 and 3 above and opposite, explain **why** John Cornwall could be accused of being **selective in the use of facts**.

Your answer must be based entirely on Sources 1, 2 and 3.

(Enquiry Skills, **8** marks)

SYLLABUS AREA 2—CHANGING SOCIETY

QUESTION 2

(*a*) *In recent years the Labour Government has introduced policies to help groups such as the unemployed and low paid workers.*

Choose **two** recent policies that have been *introduced by the Labour Government to* ***help groups such as the unemployed and low paid workers***.

Describe, **in detail**, the arguments **for** these policies.

(Knowledge and Understanding, **8** marks)

[Turn over for Question 2(*b*) on *Page six*]

QUESTION 2 (CONTINUED)

(*b*) Study the Background Information about Kwikring and Sources 1 and 2, then answer the question which follows.

Background Information about Kwikring

Kwikring is a company which deals with the telephone enquiries from customers for a whole range of businesses. It is looking to open a new call centre somewhere in Scotland. The call centre will employ 180 people, probably rising to 400 within 3 years.

The following factors will be considered when making the decision as to where the call centre will be located. **They are arranged in order of priority**.

1. Grants from central or local government.
2. A work-force which is skilled in new technology and a European language.
3. Excellent road, rail and airport links.
4. Good quality housing, education and shopping facilities for the management team moving to the area.

SOURCE 1

Information about Newtonhall

Newtonhall is a large town in East Central Scotland. It has a population of 30,000 people.

Development Assistance — A company setting up in the area would be entitled to grants from central government of up to 15% of the total costs. Newtonhall Council is in a healthy financial position and may be able to provide a little extra funding.

Education — Newtonhall has 12 Primary and 3 Secondary schools. The quality of education provided is good but several of the buildings are old and in need of repair and upgrading. There are insufficient places in local nursery schools. The local Further Education College has excellent links with local high-tech companies and uses these to develop the skills of their students. Nearby, Edinburgh provides excellent universities and a large number of private schools.

Transport — Close to the national motorway network. A major airport can be reached in 20 minutes allowing easy access to national and international flights. A mainline railway station can be reached by car in 30 minutes. The roads are congested at peak times and delays can be lengthy.

Housing/Shopping

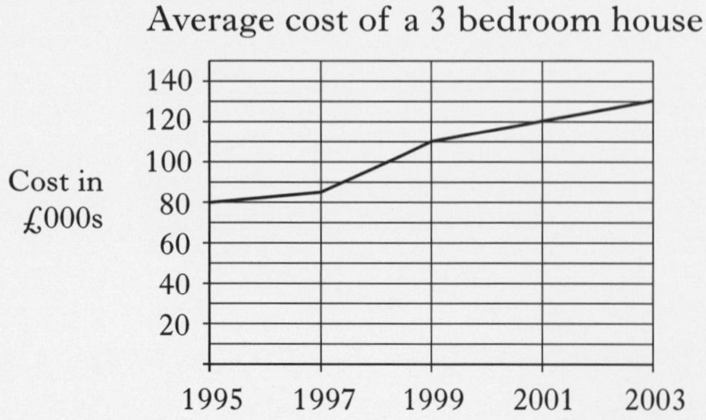

Shopping in Newtonhall	
Supermarkets	8
Out of Town Retail Parks	2
Town Centre Department Stores	3

Workforce — Several computer-related factories have closed over the last 3 years causing 1000 redundancies. Unemployment rate is 8% — well above the Scottish average.

QUESTION 2 (*b*) (CONTINUED)

SOURCE 2

Information about Inverkirk

Inverkirk is a town of 25,000 people situated in largely rural surroundings in the North East of Scotland. The nearest major city is about an hour's drive away by car.

Development Assistance — The Scottish Executive have recently increased the grant aid available to new firms setting up here to 30% of the project cost. The local council has recently overspent its budget and is unlikely to be able to provide any extra funding.

Education — All schools in the town are new. The 6 Primary schools and 2 Secondary schools have been rebuilt by the Council under a Public Private Partnership scheme. The Council have extended nursery provision and there are places available for everyone. Students who want to attend university have to travel to other towns but the local College does offer excellent foreign language courses.

Transport — There are no motorways in the area but recent road improvements mean that a major airport can be reached in less than an hour. The nearest railway station is 30 minutes away but only local trains stop there.

Housing/Shopping —

Average cost of a 3 bedroom house

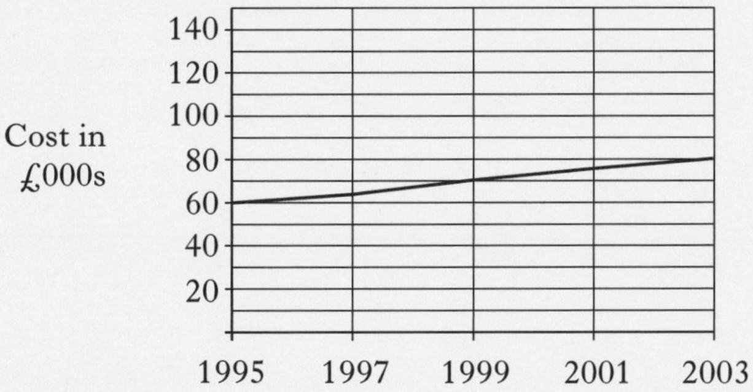

Shopping in Inverkirk	
Supermarkets	3
Out of Town Retail Parks	1
Town Centre Department Stores	0

Workforce — Last year an oil-based engineering factory closed down making 500 people redundant. A few of them are currently in training schemes learning new skills. Unemployment in the area is currently 6%.

Kwikring is considering **two** options.

Option 1 Build a call centre at Newtonhall	**Option 2** Build a call centre at Inverkirk

(i) Using only the background information and Sources 1 and 2, **explain which option you would recommend to Kwikring**.

Give **detailed** reasons to **support** your recommendation.

In your answer you must link the information about the towns to the background information about Kwikring and its priorities.

(Enquiry Skills, **8** marks)

(ii) Give **one** reason why you have **rejected** the other option.

(Enquiry Skills, **2** marks)

SYLLABUS AREA 3—IDEOLOGIES

QUESTION 3

Answer **ONE** Section only: Section (A)—The USA on pages *eight* to *eleven*.

OR Section (B)—Russia on pages *twelve* to *fifteen*.

OR Section (C)—China on pages *sixteen* to *nineteen*.

(A) **THE USA**

(*a*)

Social inequality exists in areas such as housing, health, education and the justice system in the USA.

Give **detailed** examples to show that **social** inequality exists in the USA.

In your answer you **must** refer to American examples.

(Knowledge and Understanding, **6** marks)

QUESTION 3(A) (CONTINUED)

(*b*) Study the information below, then answer the question which follows.

Public Opinion Poll — USA: State of the Union, 2002

Question: How well has George Bush performed as President?

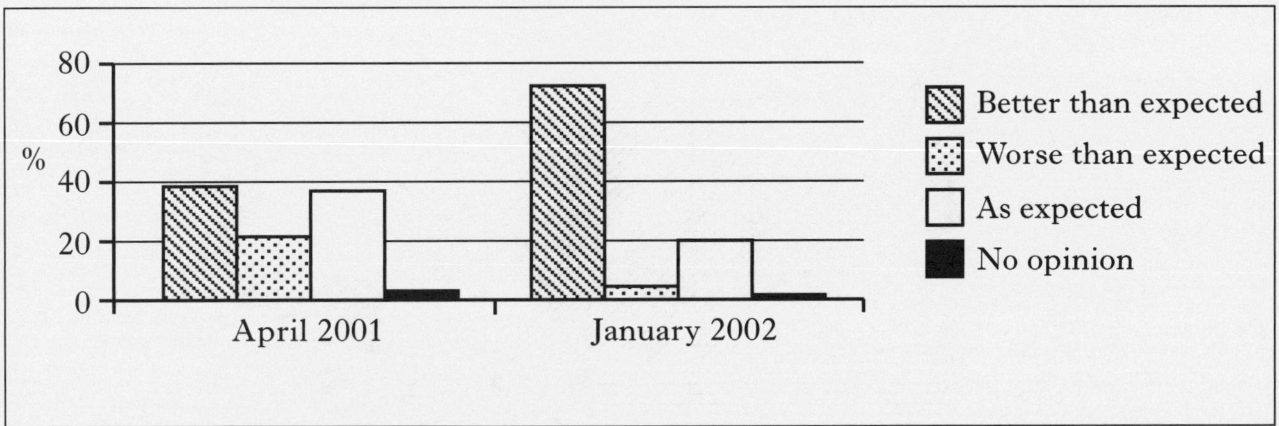

Question: Do you approve or disapprove of the way George Bush is handling the following issues?						
	Education		**Environment**		**War on Terrorism**	
	Nov 2001	Jan 2002	Nov 2001	Jan 2002	Nov 2001	Jan 2002
Approve	63%	71%	45%	54%	92%	88%
Disapprove	31%	21%	49%	31%	5%	10%
No opinion	6%	8%	6%	15%	3%	2%

Adapted from various Internet Sources

Using only the information above, what **conclusions** can be reached about George Bush's Presidency?

You must reach one **conclusion** about each of the following:

- changes in how people think George Bush has performed as President
- the issue that people feel George Bush has handled best.

(Enquiry Skills, **4** marks)

[Turn over

QUESTION 3(A) (CONTINUED)

(*c*) Study Sources 1, 2 and 3 below and opposite, then answer the question which follows.

SOURCE 1

Map of USA Showing Regions

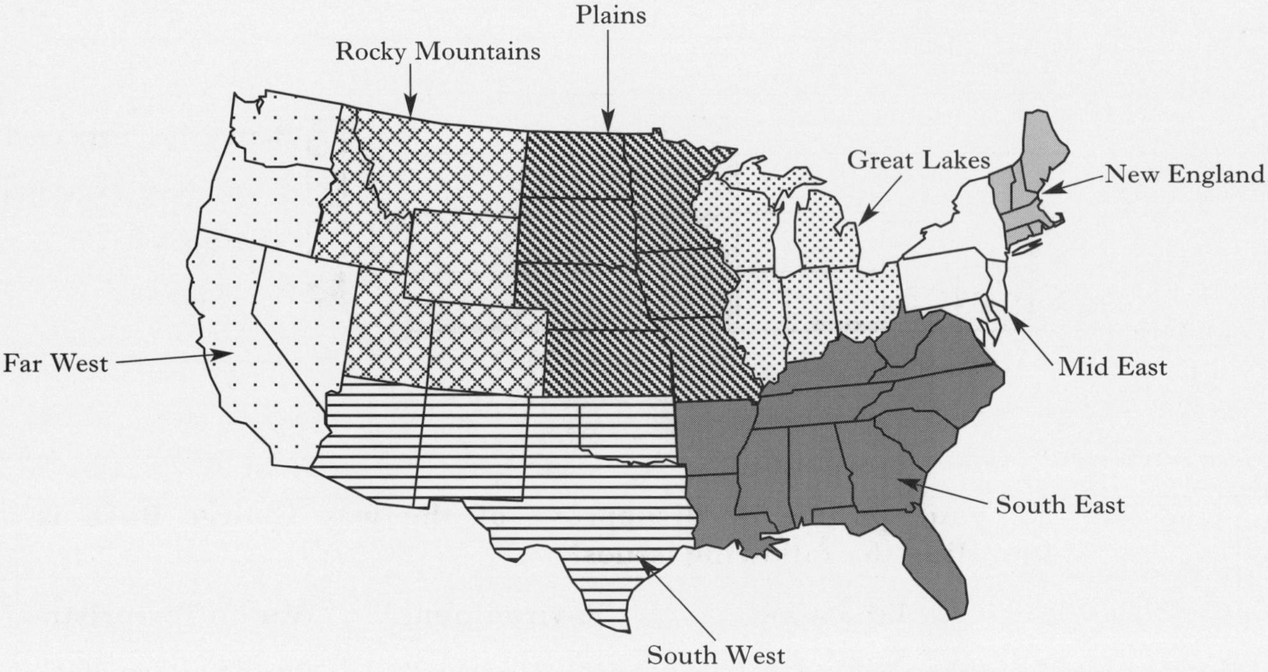

Selected Statistics of Regions of the USA

Region	Population (millions)	Per capita income (thousand dollars)	Average annual growth in income (%)	% employed in industry/ services	% employed in farming
New England	13·5	25·1	7·8	99·5	0·5
Mid East	44·8	22·9	7·2	99·3	0·7
Great Lakes	44·4	19·9	7·1	98·3	1·7
Plains	18·8	18·9	7·5	95·6	4·4
South East	66·6	17·3	8·9	98·0	2·0
South West	29·9	19·0	9·3	97·6	2·4
Rocky Mountains	8·8	19·8	9·2	97·5	2·5
Far West	45·8	22·2	8·5	98·2	1·8

QUESTION 3(A) (CONTINUED)

SOURCE 2

Statistical Information

Various Economic Indicators in the USA

	1996	1998	2000	2002
Unemployment in the USA (%)	5·6	4·6	4·0	5·6
Persons below poverty level (%)	13·7	12·7	11·3	12·9

SOURCE 3

The USA's Economy and Foreign Trade

The USA is the world's main capitalist country. The US economy began to slip into recession in August 2001. Companies in many sectors of the economy such as agriculture, mining and construction face economic decline. The US can benefit from closer trade and economic links with China.

China and the USA can become the most influential economic partnership of the new century. The USA is China's second most important trading partner. China is one of the USA's fastest-growing export markets.

Chinese statistics show that 300 of the top 500 American companies have invested in China. American companies see China as a huge market for US goods like aircraft, computers and chemical products while China supplies the USA with cheap shoes, clothes, toys and a new wave of low-cost, high-technology goods. China has agreed to cut import taxes by more than half on US agricultural products such as beef, poultry, cheese and wine. The USA will have access to China's 1·3 billion consumers and American farmers will benefit from expanded trading opportunities.

"The USA is becoming more prosperous. All American regions have similar economies. Trade with China has not helped the US economy."

View of Eddie Bernstein

Using Sources 1, 2 and 3 above and opposite, explain **why** Eddie Bernstein could be accused of being **selective in the use of facts**.

In your answer you **must** make a link between **parts of the view** and the **sources**.

(Enquiry Skills, **8** marks)

NOW GO TO QUESTION 4 ON PAGE TWENTY

QUESTION 3 (CONTINUED)

(B) **RUSSIA**

(*a*) *Social inequality exists in areas such as housing, health, education and the justice system in Russia.*

Give **detailed** examples to show that **social** inequality exists in Russia.

In your answer you **must** refer to Russian examples.

(Knowledge and Understanding, **6** marks)

QUESTION 3(B) (CONTINUED)

(*b*) Study the information below, then answer the question which follows.

Political Opinion Poll — Russia, April 2000

Question: Do you think that the Duma should have the power of veto over the president?

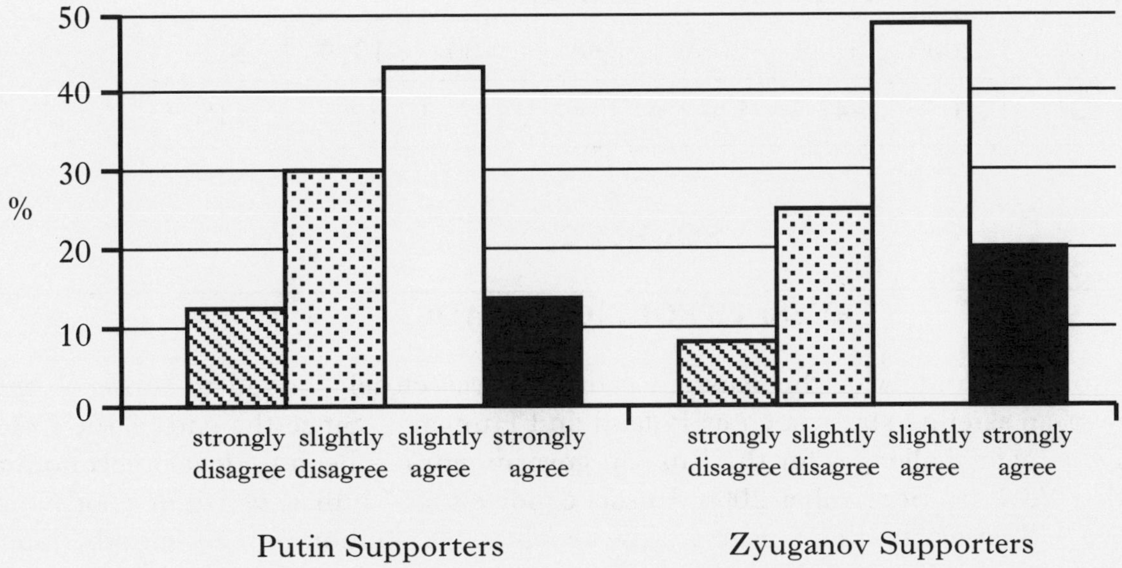

Question: What is the main issue affecting Russia at the moment? (%)

	Prices	War in Chechnya	Corruption in Government	Jobs	Health	Terrorism	Crime	Green issues
Putin Supporters	22	20	18	17	8	9	4	2
Zyuganov Supporters	33	16	19	17	9	4	1	1

Using only the information above, what **conclusions** can be reached **about differences in political opinion in Russia between Putin and Zyuganov supporters**?

You must reach one **conclusion** about each of the following:

- the power of veto
- the most urgent political issues facing the government.

(Enquiry Skills, **4** marks)

[Turn over

QUESTION 3(B) (CONTINUED)

(*c*) Study Sources 1, 2 and 3 below and opposite, then answer the question which follows.

SOURCE 1

Inflation (%)		**Industrial Output (Billion Roubles)**		**Investment in Industry (Billion Roubles)**		**Unemployment**	
1999	2000	1999	2000	1999	2000	1999	2000
36·5	1·5	442·7	520·1	114	133	12%	11%

SOURCE 2

RUSSIA'S FOREIGN TRADE

In the days of the Cold War, the Russian economy was closely linked to those of the Eastern European satellite states such as Poland and Hungary. Since the end of the Cold War, one of the main challenges for the Russian government has been to develop economic links with the West. In September 2000, Russia exported $8·7 billion worth of goods and imported $3·7 billion worth. This gave a trade surplus of $5 billion for that month alone. This took the total trade surplus for 2000 to an impressive $44·3 billion, compared to $22·9 billion for the same months in 1999.

The value of exports had risen by 47% compared to the previous year. The main exports from Russia were oil and natural gas. The world price for these was high in 2000 which was a great benefit to the Russian economy. The actual volume of exports rose slightly but their value grew significantly.

Russia's main imports are manufactured goods. The free-market economy has created greater consumer demand for household electrical goods and appliances, most of which are now imported.

There was a 9% growth from 1999 to 2000 in exports to western countries. Russian industry still struggles to compete with the west because of labour-intensive processes and out-of-date technologies. Although wage costs are low by western standards, they are not as low as in some Third World countries. Russia has not become a manufacturing base for western companies and is unlikely to become one.

QUESTION 3(B) (CONTINUED)

SOURCE 3

Russia's Regions — Population and Employment

1 Central
2 North West
3 South
4 Privolzhsky
5 Urals
6 Siberia
7 Far East

	Urban Population (%)	Rural Population (%)	Percentage of population who are working age	Percentage Employed in industry	Percentage employed in farming
Central	79	21	59	21	11
North West	81	19	62	23	6
South	57	43	58	18	22
Privolzhsky	71	29	60	25	16
Urals	80	20	62	26	9
Siberia	70	30	61	22	14
Far East	76	24	65	20	8

"The Russian economy is becoming more prosperous. All regions have a similar employment pattern. Russia's foreign trade shows signs of growth."

View of Olga Yurana, economics correspondent for newspaper

Using Sources 1, 2 and 3 above and opposite, explain **why** Olga Yurana could be accused of being **selective in the use of facts**.

In your answer you **must** make a link between **parts of the view** and the **sources**.

(Enquiry Skills, **8** marks)

NOW GO TO QUESTION 4 ON PAGE TWENTY

QUESTION 3 (CONTINUED)

(C) **CHINA**

(*a*)

Social inequality exists in areas such as housing, health, education and the justice system in China.

Give **detailed** examples to show that **social** inequality exists in China.

In your answer you **must** refer to Chinese examples.

(Knowledge and Understanding, **6** marks)

QUESTION 3 (C) (CONTINUED)

(*b*) Study the information below, then answer the question which follows.

Information about Education in China

Number of Teachers (millions)

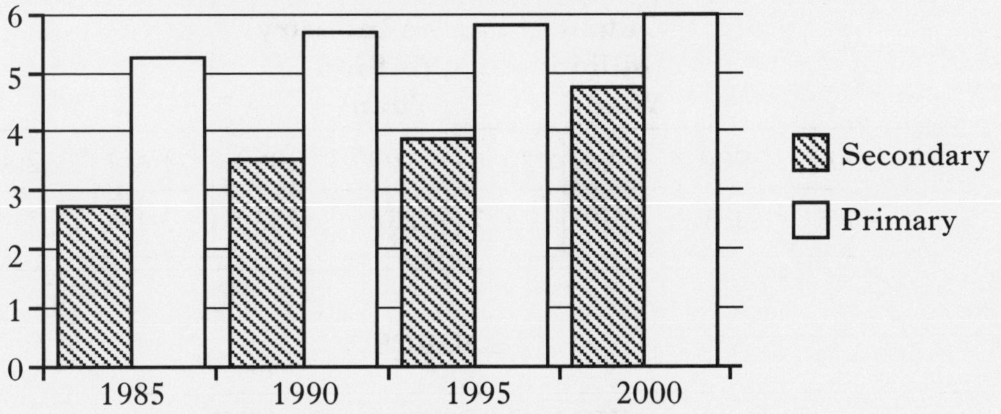

Number of Students (millions)

	1985	**1990**	**1995**	**2000**
Universities	1·7	2·1	2·9	5·6
Secondary Schools	50·0	51·1	61·9	83·6
Primary Schools	133·7	122·4	131·9	130·1
Nursery Schools	14·7	19·7	27·1	23·2

Using only the information above, what **conclusions** can be reached about **changes** in Education in China?

You **must** reach one **conclusion** about each of the following:

- the number of teachers in different types of educational establishments
- the number of students in education at different levels.

(Enquiry Skills, **4** marks)

[Turn over

QUESTION 3 (C) (CONTINUED)

(*c*) Study Sources 1, 2 and 3 below and opposite, then answer the question which follows.

SOURCE 1

Inflation (%)		**Industrial Output (Billion Yuan)**		**Investment in Industry (Billion Yuan)**		**Unemployment**	
1999	2000	1999	2000	1999	2000	1999	2000
–1·5	–1·3	6779	7477	2366	2530	3·1%	3·1%

SOURCE 2

CHINA'S FOREIGN TRADE

In recent years, China has greatly increased its involvement in foreign trade. One aspect of this has been the establishment of China as a manufacturing centre for multi-national businesses. Because wages are low and there is a large supply of skilled workers, China is an attractive country for manufacturers.

In 2001, China claimed that it was the world's largest exporter of Christmas products. The state-run news agency claimed that seven out of every ten artificial Christmas trees bought by Americans were made in the southern Chinese city of Shenzhen. The agency said that the city earns $100 million annually from artificial Christmas trees alone. The city has 20 factories specialising in the trees and about 300 in total dedicated to producing Christmas products.

China's Special Economic Zones have helped it to become a major force in the world economy. Businesses are attracted to them because of incentives. This in turn creates jobs and boosts the local economy.

China has had to alter some of its political principles to become a major economic power. The centres of major cities such as Beijing and Shanghai now have branches of many western shops and businesses.

QUESTION 3 (C) (*c*) (CONTINUED)

SOURCE 3

Statistics for selected Chinese Cities

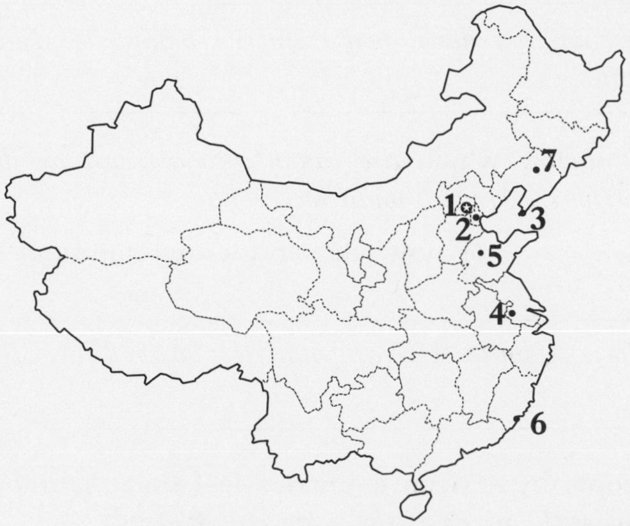

1 Beijing
2 Tianjin
3 Dalian
4 Jinan
5 Nanjing
6 Xiamen
7 Shenyang

	Average number of persons per household	**Average number of employees per household**	**Average number of children per employee**	**Per capita monthly income (Yuan)**	**Per capita monthly disposable income (Yuan)**
Beijing	3·1	1·7	1·8	709·3	704·8
Tianjin	3·1	1·6	1·9	689·9	686·1
Dalian	3·2	1·4	2·2	597·7	591·9
Nanjing	2·9	1·6	1·8	692·2	690·1
Jinan	3·0	1·8	1·7	695·7	690·7
Xiamen	3·2	1·8	1·8	989·6	985·9
Shenyang	3·3	1·8	1·8	1800·3	1786·6

"The Chinese economy is becoming more prosperous. All cities in China are equally prosperous. Foreign trade is one of the less successful aspects of the economy."

View of Li Rongji, economics correspondent for newspaper

Using Sources 1, 2 and 3 above and opposite, explain **why** Li Rongji could be accused of being **selective in the use of facts**.

In your answer you **must** make a link between **parts of the view** and the **sources**.

(Enquiry Skills, **8** marks)

NOW GO TO QUESTION 4 ON PAGE TWENTY

SYLLABUS AREA 4—INTERNATIONAL RELATIONS

QUESTION 4

(*a*)

> *Political factors are taken into account by developed countries before deciding which countries in Africa should receive aid.*

Describe, **in detail**, the *political factors* which *are taken into account by developed countries before deciding which countries in Africa should receive aid.*

(Knowledge and Understanding, **4** marks)

(*b*)

> *Some people feel that the aid which is given to African countries does not meet the needs of the majority of people.*

Explain, **in detail**, why some people in African countries feel that *the aid which is given to African countries does not meet the needs of the majority of people.*

(Knowledge and Understanding, **4** marks)

QUESTION 4 (CONTINUED)

You have been asked to carry out an investigation on the topic below.

The work of the United Nations in Africa

Now answer questions (*c*), (*d*), (*e*) and (*f*).

(*c*) State a relevant **hypothesis** for your investigation.

(Enquiry Skills, **2** marks)

(*d*) Give **two** relevant **aims or headings** to help you prove or disprove your hypothesis.

(Enquiry Skills, **2** marks)

(*e*) Study the Web site Homepage of the United Nations below, then answer the question which follows.

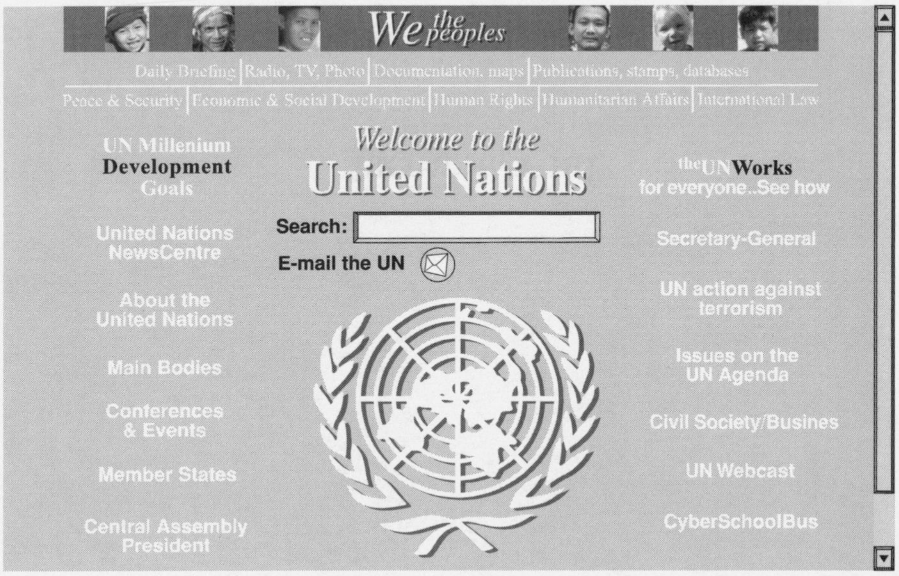

Describe, in detail, how you would use the **Homepage of the United Nations** in your investigation.

(Enquiry Skills, **2** marks)

(*f*) Explain, **in detail**, **two** ways in which visiting a **library** might be useful for your investigation.

(Enquiry Skills, **4** marks)

[*END OF QUESTION PAPER*]

[BLANK PAGE]

[BLANK PAGE]

G

2640/402

NATIONAL QUALIFICATIONS 2004

MONDAY, 24 MAY
10.20 AM–11.50 AM

MODERN STUDIES
STANDARD GRADE
General Level

1 Read every question carefully.

2 Answer all questions as fully as you can.

3 If you cannot do a question, go on to the next one. Try again later.

4 In question 3, answer **one** section only; Section (A) The USA or Section (B) Russia or Section (C) China.

5 Write your answers in the answer book provided. Indicate clearly, in the left hand margin, the question and section of question being answered. Do not write in the right hand margin.

SCOTTISH QUALIFICATIONS AUTHORITY

THB 2640/402 6/22620

SYLLABUS AREA 1—LIVING IN A DEMOCRACY

QUESTION 1

(*a*)

> *Trade union members can support their union during a dispute.*

Describe **two** actions which *trade union members can take to support their union during a dispute.*

(Knowledge and Understanding, **4** marks)

(*b*) Study Sources 1 and 2 below, then answer the question which follows.

SOURCE 1

Information about Glenmarsh Textile Factory

Glenmarsh textile factory has lost orders from all over the world. The management wants to cut hours and pay, and to introduce retraining schemes for the workers. The Shop Steward has resigned. Negotiations with the workers are about to start. The new Shop Steward will also have to discuss safety concerns after an accident at the factory and a complaint by two female workers that they have been treated unfairly.

SOURCE 2

Sheila Cameron

Sheila is 55 years old and has worked at Glenmarsh for 12 years. In 1999, she completed a Health and Safety course at union headquarters. She wants to protect the jobs and pay of the workers. In previous disputes she has been a good negotiator. She is very popular with the workers.

Davie Paterson

Davie Paterson is regarded as an expert in dealing with sex discrimination cases. He also has experience of retraining schemes and spoke to the TUC conference about ways to introduce these to companies. He is 54 years old and has worked at Glenmarsh for 10 years.

Using only the information in Sources 1 and 2 above, **explain which person would be the better choice as the Shop Steward** for the workers at Glenmarsh Textiles.

Give **two** reasons for your choice.

You **must** link the information in Source 1 to the person you have chosen.

(Enquiry Skills, **4** marks)

QUESTION 1 (CONTINUED)

(*c*)

MSPs work on behalf of the people they represent.

Describe **one** way in which MSPs find out about problems in their local area.

AND

Describe **one** thing the MSP could do to draw attention to problems in his/her local area.

(Knowledge and Understanding, **4** marks)

(*d*) Study the information below, then answer the question which follows.

Support for Selected Political Parties in Opinion Polls

	Conservative	*Labour*	*Liberal Democrat*
2000	34%	44%	17%
2001	30%	46%	17%
2002	32%	41%	21%

Source: ICM Polls

Write down **two** conclusions about support for political parties in the Opinion Polls shown.

You must only use the information above.

(Enquiry Skills, **4** marks)

[Turn over

SYLLABUS AREA 2—CHANGING SOCIETY

QUESTION 2

(*a*)

The Government tries to help unemployed people find work.

Describe **two** ways in which *the Government tries to help unemployed people find work.*

(Knowledge and Understanding, **4** marks)

(*b*)

Some people need to receive benefits from the government.

Apart from unemployment, give **two** reasons why *some people need to receive benefits from the government.*

(Knowledge and Understanding, **4** marks)

(*c*) Study Sources 1 and 2 below and opposite, then answer the question which follows.

SOURCE 1

UK Female Unemployment Rates 1990–2000 (Selected Groups)		
	1990	*2000*
White	6%	5%
Indian	11%	9%
Pakistani/Bangladeshi	25%	21%
African/Caribbean	10%	14%

QUESTION 2 (*c*) (CONTINUED)

SOURCE 2

Average Weekly Earnings (£)—UK Females 2001

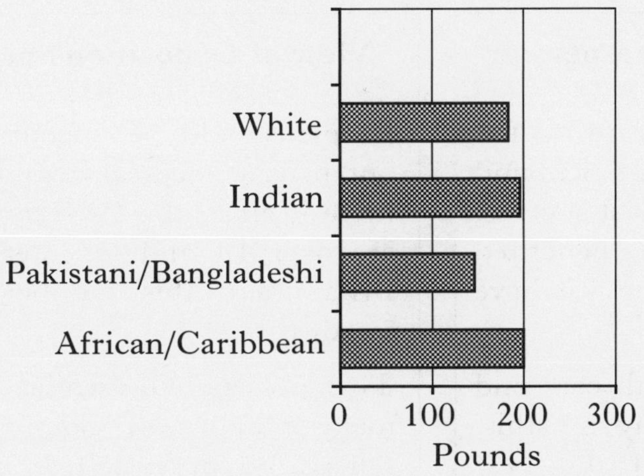

Statements by Sandeep Kholi

- In 2001, white women earned more than all the other female groups.
- The unemployment rate for Indian women fell between 1990 and 2000.
- In 2001, African/Caribbean women earned more than Pakistani/Bangladeshi women.
- All women have similar rates of unemployment.

Using **only** Sources 1 and 2 above, write down **two** statements made by Sandeep Kholi that are **exaggerated**.

Using the statistics in the Sources, give **one** reason why **each** of the statements you have chosen is **exaggerated**.

(Enquiry Skills, **4** marks)

[Turn over

QUESTION 2 (CONTINUED)

(*d*) Study Sources 1 and 2 below, then answer the question which follows.

SOURCE 1

View of Government Spokesperson

Free personal and nursing care for the elderly has been available in Scotland since 2002. It has been a great success. Over 75 000 older people have benefited from the extra £150 million we have spent each year.

People have a right to health care and the Government should pay for this. Our elderly people expect the best treatment and this is what we will give them.

SOURCE 2

View of Opposition Spokesperson

People should be encouraged to take out private medical insurance and not leave it all to the Government. There are over 10 million elderly people in Britain and this number is growing steadily.

The present Government has spent many millions of pounds on a new scheme to provide free personal and nursing care, but this has not worked well.

Sources 1 and 2 give **different** views about **health care for elderly people**.

Write down **two** differences between these views.

You must use only information from the Sources above.

(Enquiry Skills, **4** marks)

SYLLABUS AREA 3—IDEOLOGIES

QUESTION 3

Answer **ONE** section only: Section (A)—The USA on pages seven and eight

OR Section (B)—Russia on pages nine and ten

OR Section (C)—China on pages eleven and twelve

(A) **THE USA**

(*a*)

Education	**Housing**	**Health**

Choose **one** of the topics from the box above.

Give **two** reasons why some members of **ethnic minority groups** often do less well than white Americans in the topic you have chosen.

In your answer, you must refer to ethnic minority groups in the USA that you have studied.

(Knowledge & Understanding, **4** marks)

(*b*) Study Sources 1 and 2 below, then answer the question which follows.

SOURCE 1

Economic Statistics—USA

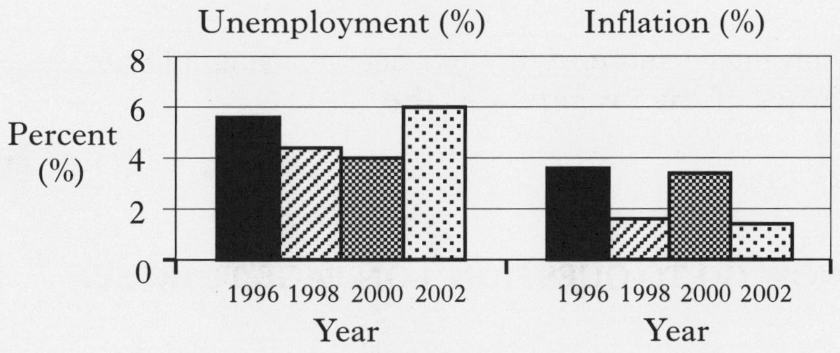

SOURCE 2

Newspaper Report—Industry in the USA

Industrial production in the USA has fallen for the first time in eight years. The terrorist attacks of September 11th 2001 have caused many problems. These have affected American business badly and put industry under great pressure.

The import of cheap goods from other countries like China is also a problem. People are buying imported clothing and electrical goods instead of products made in the USA. These problems have caused share prices to fall.

Unemployment is an increasing problem in the USA. American industry has suffered due to competition from abroad.

View of a Democrat Senator

Using **only** Sources 1 and 2 above, give **two** reasons to **support** the view of the Democrat Senator.

Your answer must be based entirely on the sources above.

(Enquiry Skills, **4** marks)

QUESTION 3 (A) (CONTINUED)

You are investigating the topic in the box below.

The work of the President of the USA

Answer questions (*c*), (*d*) and (*e*) which follow.

(*c*) As part of the **planning stage** of your investigation, give **two** relevant aims for your investigation.

(Enquiry Skills, **2** marks)

(*d*) You decide to use the **Internet** to gather information about **the work of the President of the USA**.

Give **two** ways in which you could use the Internet to help with your investigation.

(Enquiry Skills, **2** marks)

You also decide to use a **library** as a source for your investigation.

(*e*) Describe **one** advantage and **one** disadvantage of using a library as a source to find out about **the work of the President of the USA**.

(Enquiry Skills, **4** marks)

NOW GO TO QUESTION 4 ON PAGE THIRTEEN

QUESTION 3 (CONTINUED)

(B) **RUSSIA**

(*a*)

Education	**Housing**	**Health**

Choose **one** of the topics from the box above.

Give **two** reasons why some Russians are better off than others in the topic you have chosen.

(Knowledge & Understanding, **4** marks)

(*b*) Study Sources 1 and 2 below, then answer the question which follows.

SOURCE 1

Economic Statistics—Russia

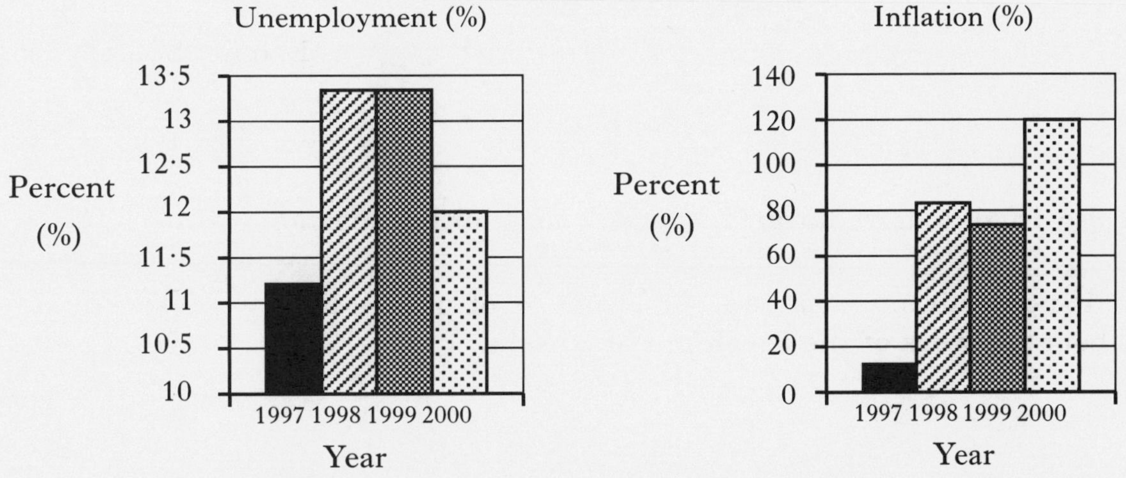

SOURCE 2

Newspaper Report—Industry in Russia

Russian industry has suffered from a lack of investment over the past twenty years. This means that the methods of production are now out-of-date by world standards. Russian industry tends to rely on large numbers of workers. New technology is not as common as in other parts of the world.

Costs of production are high. Because of this, Russia has not been able to attract foreign companies to use the country as a manufacturing centre.

Inflation is an increasing problem in Russia. Russian industry is "old fashioned" compared to the rest of the world.

View of a Communist Deputy

Using **only** Sources 1 and 2 above, give **two** reasons to **support** the view of the Communist Deputy.

(Enquiry Skills, **4** marks)

QUESTION 3 (B) (CONTINUED)

You are investigating the topic in the box below.

The work of the President of Russia

Answer questions (*c*), (*d*) and (*e*) which follow.

(*c*) As part of the **planning stage** of your investigation, give **two** relevant aims for your investigation.

(Enquiry Skills, **2** marks)

(*d*) You decide to use the **Internet** to gather information about **the work of the President of Russia**.

Give **two** ways in which you could use the Internet to help with your investigation.

(Enquiry Skills, **2** marks)

You also decide to use a **library** as a source for your investigation.

(*e*) Describe **one** advantage and **one** disadvantage of using a library as a source to find out about **the work of the President of Russia**.

(Enquiry Skills, **4** marks)

NOW GO ON TO QUESTION 4 ON PAGE THIRTEEN

QUESTION 3 (CONTINUED)

(C) **CHINA**

(*a*)

Education	**Housing**	**Health**

Choose **one** of the topics from the box above.

Give **two** reasons why some Chinese people are better off than others in the topic you have chosen.

(Knowledge & Understanding, **4** marks)

(*b*) Study Sources 1 and 2 below, then answer the question which follows.

SOURCE 1

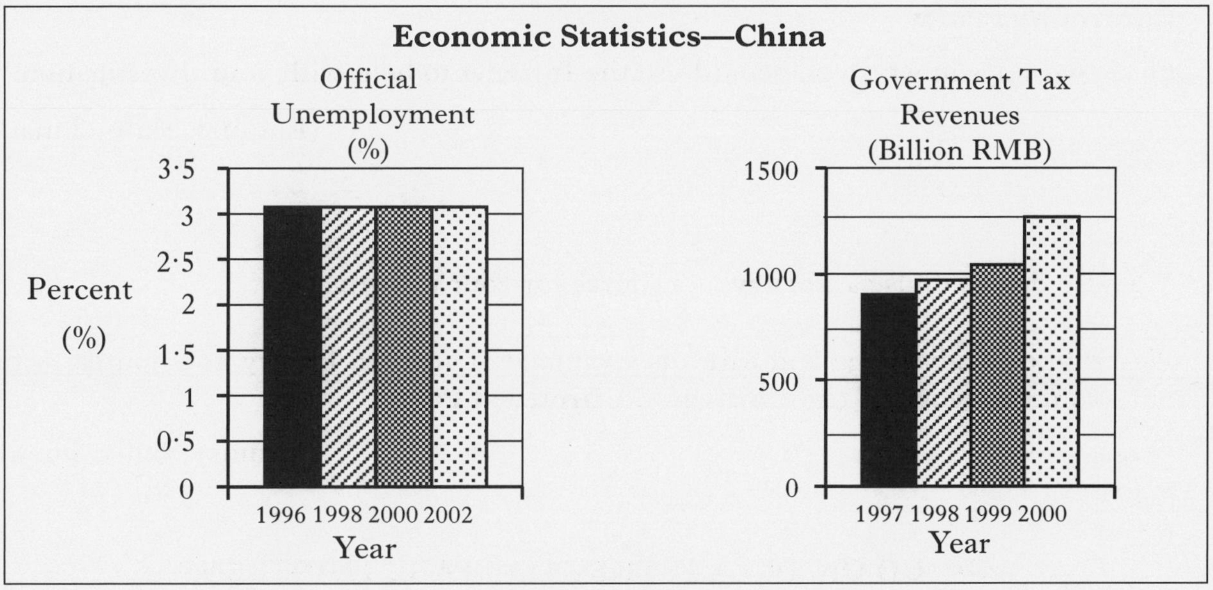

SOURCE 2

Newspaper Report—Industry in China

Much of Chinese industry is still state-owned. However, a more competitive market has been introduced meaning that factories must be efficient and make good use of resources. Many Chinese industries now act as a manufacturing centre for foreign countries—China's low wage costs and cheaper production make it attractive.

The links between Chinese industry and the prison camp system are controversial. Some factories use convicted prisoners as their labour force.

Official unemployment rates in China show little change over the years. Chinese industry has benefited from contact with the outside world.

View of a Communist Deputy

Using **only** Sources 1 and 2 above, give **two** reasons to **support** the view of the Communist Deputy.

Your answer must be based entirely on the sources above.

(Enquiry Skills, **4** marks)

QUESTION 3 (C) (CONTINUED)

You are investigating the topic in the box below.

The work of the Chinese Communist Party

Answer questions (*c*), (*d*) and (*e*) which follow.

(*c*) As part of the **planning stage** of your investigation, give **two** relevant aims for your investigation.

(Enquiry Skills, **2** marks)

(*d*) You decide to use the Internet to gather information about **the work of the Chinese Communist Party**.

Give **two** ways in which you could use the Internet to help with your investigation.

(Enquiry Skills, **2** marks)

You also decide to use a **library** as a source for your investigation.

(*e*) Describe **one** advantage and **one** disadvantage of using a library as a source to find out about **the work of the Chinese Communist Party**.

(Enquiry Skills, **4** marks)

NOW GO ON TO QUESTION 4 ON PAGE THIRTEEN

SYLLABUS AREA 4—INTERNATIONAL RELATIONS

QUESTION 4

(*a*)

United Nations Specialised Agencies

UNICEF **WHO**

Choose **one** of the UN Specialised Agencies shown above.

Describe **two** ways in which the Agency you have chosen tries to meet the needs of many people in Africa.

(Knowledge and Understanding, **4** marks)

(*b*)

In 2003, the United Kingdom gave farming equipment to several African countries as part of an aid package.

Give **two** reasons why the UK may benefit from giving aid to African countries.

(Knowledge and Understanding, **4** marks)

[Turn over

QUESTION 4 (CONTINUED)

(*c*) Study the information below and then answer the question which follows.

Timeline—Zimbabwe	
Key Events 2000–2002	
Date	**Event**
February 2000	With the support of the Government, blacks seize hundreds of farms owned by whites. This is part of a campaign to take back land they believe was stolen from them by white farmers.
July 2001	Zimbabwe facing massive food shortages.
February 2002	All European Union countries cut trade links with Zimbabwe because of land policy.
April 2002	Very little food available legally but it can easily be bought on the "black market". However, "black market" prices are four times the normal rate.
May 2002	Worsening food shortages turning into a famine. The World Food Programme blames the land policy for this.
June 2002	2900 white farmers ordered to stop working and to leave within 45 days.

Adapted from BBC website

Statements made in a speech by Khalif–al–Toure

- The Government of Zimbabwe has helped white farmers.
- World Food Programme blames the land policy for the famine in Zimbabwe.
- It is only the UK government which has cut trade links because of the changing land policy.
- Food is available on the "black market" but it is very expensive.

Using **only** the information above, write down **two** statements by Khalif-al-Toure which are **exaggerated**.

Using the Timeline, give **one** reason why each of the statements you have chosen is **exaggerated**.

You must only use the information above.

(Enquiry Skills, **4** marks)

QUESTION 4 (CONTINUED)

(*d*) Study the information below then answer the question which follows.

Southern African Famine, 2002–2003

	July 2002		**March 2003**	
	Affected by famine		*Affected by famine*	
	Number	*% of Population*	*Number*	*% of Population*
Angola	1·0 million	10	1·5 million	15
Malawi	0·5 million	5	3·2 million	30
Mozambique	0·4 million	2	0·5 million	3
Zambia	1·3 million	12	2·4 million	25
Zimbabwe	5·3 million	47	6·1 million	54

Write down **two conclusions** that can be reached about the famine in Southern Africa.

You should write **one** conclusion about **each** of the following.

- The country worst affected by famine in July 2002
- The changes that have taken place in the countries affected by famine between July 2002 and March 2003

Your conclusions must be based entirely on the information above.

(Enquiry Skills, **4** marks)

[*END OF QUESTION PAPER*]

[BLANK PAGE]

2004 | Credit

[BLANK PAGE]

C

2640/403

NATIONAL QUALIFICATIONS 2004

MONDAY, 24 MAY
1.00 PM – 3.00 PM

MODERN STUDIES
STANDARD GRADE
Credit Level

1 Read every question carefully.

2 Answer all questions as fully as you can.

3 If you cannot do a question, go on to the next one. Try again later.

4 In question 3, answer **one** section only: Section (A) The USA **or** Section (B) Russia **or** Section (C) China.

5 Write your answers in the answer book provided. Indicate clearly, in the left hand margin, the question and section of question being answered. Do not write in the right hand margin.

SCOTTISH QUALIFICATIONS AUTHORITY

SYLLABUS AREA 1—LIVING IN A DEMOCRACY

QUESTION 1

(*a*) *Pressure groups in the UK have* ***rights and responsibilities*** *in any actions they take in trying to influence public opinion and Government policy.*

Describe, **in detail**, the **rights and responsibilities** of pressure groups.

Answers **must** refer to specific Pressure Groups you have studied.

(Knowledge & Understanding, **8** marks)

(*b*) Study the cartoon below, then answer the question which follows.

Using **only** the cartoon above, what **conclusions** can be reached about the attitudes of people towards elections?

You must reach **two** separate conclusions.

Enquiry Skills, **4** marks)

QUESTION 1 (CONTINUED)

(*c*) Study the information below, then answer the question which follows.

Average Number of Parliamentary Questions Asked By Each MSP in the Scottish Parliament (By Party) — 2001

Oral Questions

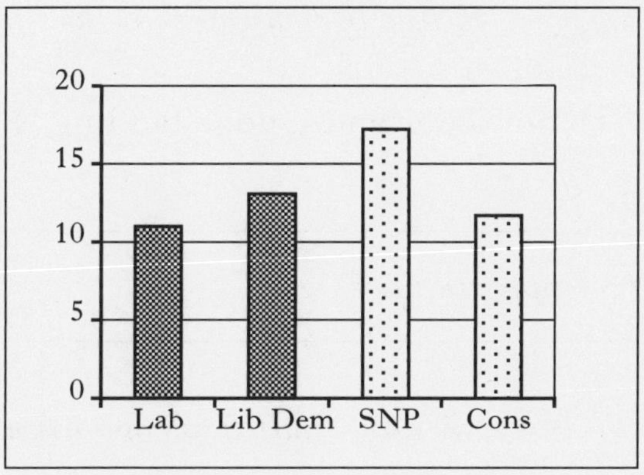

Written Questions

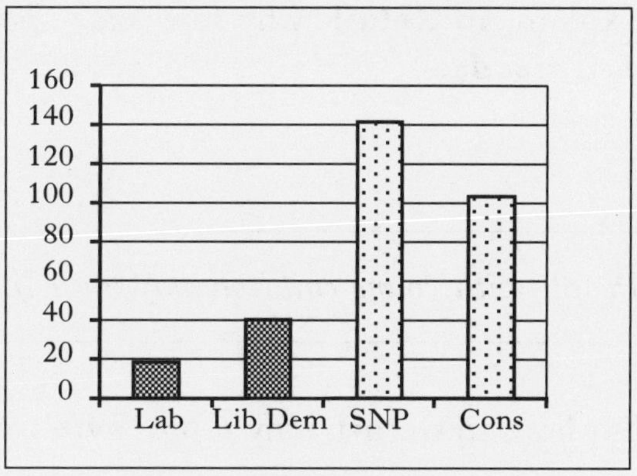

First Minister's Questions

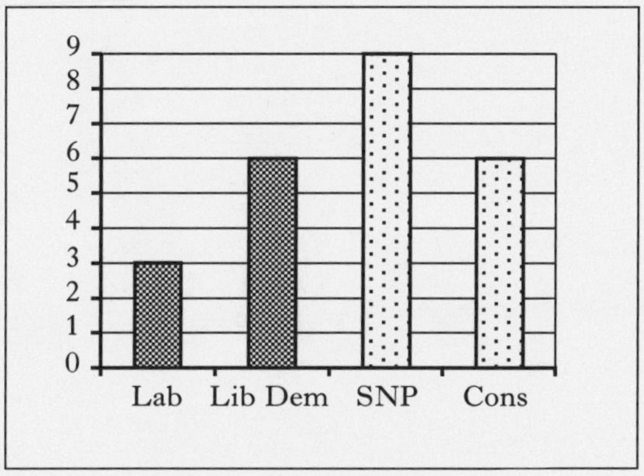

Composition of the Scottish Parliament

Party	MSPs
Executive Coalition Parties	
Labour/Lib Dem	72
Opposition Parties	
SNP	34
Conservative	19
Others	4

The main opposition party asks more Parliamentary Questions than the Executive Coalition parties put together.

View of Willie McKay

Give **one** reason to **support** and **one** reason to **oppose** the view of Willie McKay.

Overall, do you agree with Willie McKay? **Explain your answer**.

(Enquiry Skills, **6** marks)

[Turn over

SYLLABUS AREA 2—CHANGING SOCIETY

QUESTION 2

(*a*) | *Some older people in the UK live in housing that does not meet their* ***needs***.

Explain, **in detail**, why *some older people in the UK live in housing that does not meet their* ***needs***.

(Knowledge and Understanding, **4** marks)

(*b*) | *People with young children may have limited job opportunities.*

Explain, **in detail**, why *people with young children may have limited job opportunities.*

(Knowledge and Understanding, **4** marks)

QUESTION 2 (CONTINUED)

You have been asked to carry out an investigation into the topic in the box below.

Changing technology and work.

Now answer questions (*c*), (*d*), (*e*) and (*f*).

(*c*) State a relevant **hypothesis** for your investigation.

(Enquiry Skills, **2** marks)

(*d*) Give **two** relevant **aims** or **headings** to help you prove or disprove your hypothesis.

(Enquiry Skills, **2** marks)

To help with your investigation you decide to **interview** the manager of a local factory.

(*e*) Describe the steps you would take to **arrange a visit** to the factory to conduct your interview.

(Enquiry Skills, **2** marks)

(*f*) Describe, **in detail**, the **advantages and disadvantages** of **interviewing** the manager as a method for your investigation.

(Enquiry Skills, **4** marks)

[Turn over

[BLANK PAGE]

SYLLABUS AREA 3—IDEOLOGIES

QUESTION 3

Answer **one** section only: Section (A) — The USA on pages *seven* to *ten*
OR Section (B) — Russia on pages *eleven* to *fourteen*
OR Section (C) — China on pages *fifteen* to *eighteen*

(A) THE USA

(*a*) *American citizens can participate in elections.*

Describe, **in detail**, the ways in which *American citizens can participate in elections.*

In your answer you **must** refer to American examples of participation in elections.

(Knowledge and Understanding, **8** marks)

[Turn over

QUESTION 3 (A) (CONTINUED)

(*b*) Study the information below, then answer the question which follows on page *nine*.

HEALTH IN THE USA — A RECORD TO BE PROUD OF?

Good health and equality of health are important in a modern country. Between 1900 and 2000, life expectancy in the USA increased from 51 to 80 for females and from 48 to 74 for males. The Census Bureau estimates that life expectancy will be 87 for females and 81 for males by 2050.

One criticism of the health record of the USA is the link between poor health and factors such as education and gender. Men continue to have a worse death rate than women, and women have lower mortality rates at every age. Mortality rates improved more for women than for men. The gender gap in life expectancy actually increased. The number of years of education is also important. Men who have under 12 years of education have a death rate of 764 per 100 000 but if they have more than 13 years of education the death rate drops to 264. The pattern for women is similar — 410 and 173 per 100 000 depending on the number of years of education.

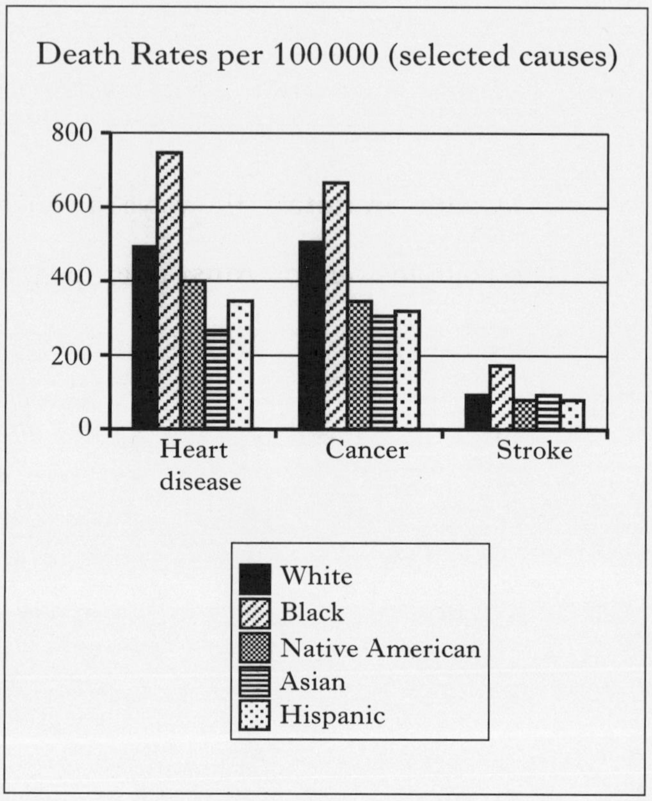

Death Rates per 100 000 People in the USA

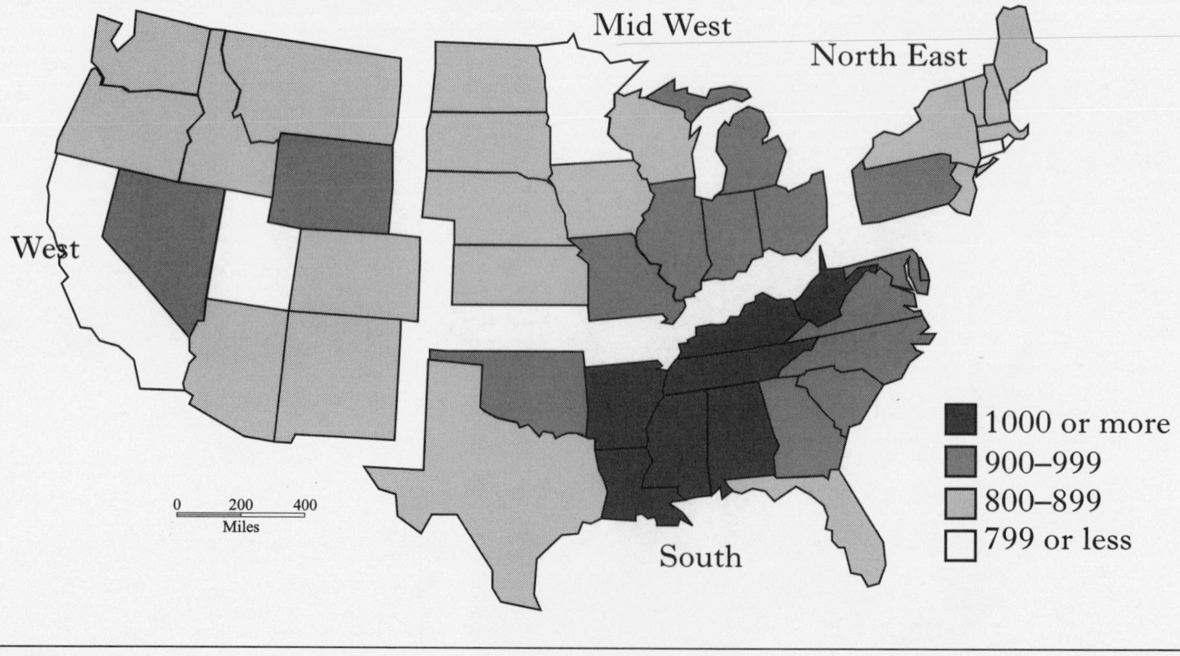

QUESTION 3 (A) (*b*) (CONTINUED)

Location, education and race have little effect on health in the USA.

View of Hilary Wallace

Using **only** the information on page *eight*, explain **the extent to which** Hilary Wallace could be accused of being **selective in the use of facts**.

(Enquiry Skills, **6** marks)

[Turn over

QUESTION 3 (A) (CONTINUED)

(*c*) Study the information below, then answer the question which follows.

Selected Information on Asian Immigration to the USA

Region	**Where recent immigrants have settled (%)**	**Average Hourly Earnings ($)**	**Percentage of the population who are Asian**	**US–Asian owned firms (%)***
New England	3	17·5	2·7	2·4
Middle Atlantic	22	18·7	4·4	19·8
East North Central	8	16·1	2·0	7·5
West North Central	2	15·0	1·6	1·8
South Atlantic	15	15·2	2·1	12·4
East South Central	1	15·0	0·8	1·5
West South Central	11	15·1	2·2	7·9
Mountain	4	14·7	1·9	3·1
Pacific	34	17·7	10·3	43·6

*This column refers to the percentage of all businesses owned by US–Asians that are located in each region.

Using **only** the information above, give **two** conclusions about the reasons why recent Asian immigrants are more likely to settle in certain regions of the USA.

(Enquiry Skills, **4** marks)

NOW GO TO QUESTION 4 ON PAGE NINETEEN

QUESTION 3 (CONTINUED)

(B) **RUSSIA**

(*a*) *Russian citizens can participate in elections.*

Describe, **in detail**, the ways in which *Russian citizens can participate in elections.*

In your answer you **must** refer to Russian examples of participation in elections.

(Knowledge and Understanding, **8** marks)

[Turn over

QUESTION 3 (B) (CONTINUED)

(*b*) Study the information below, then answer the question which follows on page *thirteen*.

CRISIS FOR HEALTH STANDARDS IN RUSSIA

The Soviet Union broke up into several independent states in the early 1990s. These include Russia, Belarus, Ukraine and Estonia. The system of health care in Russia is in danger of collapsing. Back in the Communist period, hospitals and health care were generously funded with large state subsidies. Now, in the free-market economy, health care has been starved of resources. A system that was the envy of the rest of the world has become a source of shame.

The standard of health care a person can expect varies depending on where they live. People from major cities such as Moscow and St Petersburg enjoy a level of care that is better than anywhere in the whole of the former Soviet Union. However, in remote areas of the north and east of Russia, health care standards are very poor. In the far east of Russia some people live more than 200 miles from the nearest hospital.

Medical services in countries such as Estonia, Ukraine and Belarus have benefited from closer links with Europe. Russia has been slower to make these links and standards have suffered.

Selected Causes of Death in 4 former Soviet States (per 1000 people)

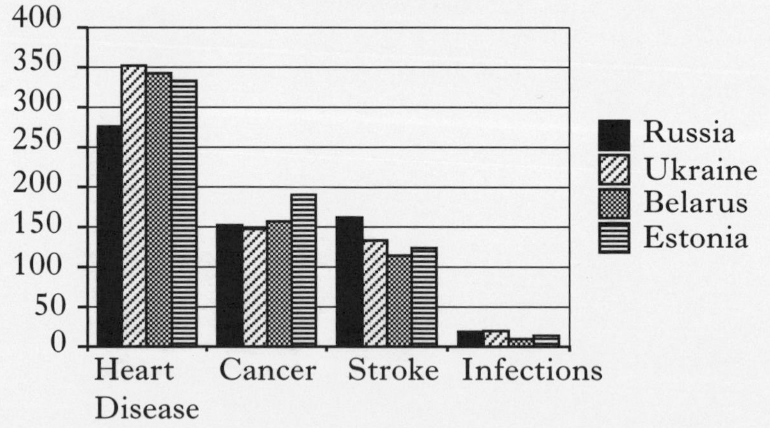

Health-related Statistics in 4 former Soviet States

	Crude Death Rate (per 1000 people)	Life Expectancy at Birth	Mothers who die in childbirth (per 100 000 births)	Infant Mortality rate (per 1000 births)
Russia	16	65	75	15
Ukraine	15	68	45	12
Belarus	14	69	33	9
Estonia	14	71	80	9

QUESTION 3 (B) (*b*) (CONTINUED)

Health standards in Russia are worse than in other former Soviet states.

View of Olga Davidova

Using **only** the information on page *twelve*, explain **the extent to which** Olga Davidova could be accused of being **selective in the use of facts**.

(Enquiry Skills, **6** marks)

[Turn over

QUESTION 3 (B) (CONTINUED)

(*c*) Study the information below then answer the question which follows.

Selected Information on Education in autonomous Republics within Russia

Republic	**Population (million)**	**Number of General Schools**	**Number of Vocational Schools**	**Number of Higher Schools**
Bashkortostan	4·0	3264	157	9
Buryatia	1·1	602	44	4
Chuvashia	1·4	715	35	3
Dagestan	2·1	1589	29	5
Karelia	0·8	336	21	3
Komi	1·2	591	12	1
Sakha	1·1	711	33	2
Tatarstan	3·8	2422	118	15
Udmurtia	1·5	882	45	15

Using **only** the information above, give **two** conclusions about the provision of different types of school in the autonomous republics.

(Enquiry Skills, **4** marks)

NOW GO TO QUESTION 4 ON PAGE NINETEEN

QUESTION 3 (CONTINUED)

(C) **CHINA**

(*a*) | *Chinese citizens would like more freedom to participate in elections.* |

Describe, **in detail**, the ways in which *Chinese citizens could participate more fully in elections if they were given more freedom*.

In your answer you **must** refer to Chinese examples.

(Knowledge and Understanding, **8** marks)

[Turn over

QUESTION 3 (C) (CONTINUED)

(*b*) Study the information below, then answer the question which follows on page *seventeen*.

EDUCATION IN CHINA — A RECORD TO BE PROUD OF?

In 1990, the average class size for secondary schools was 15 and for primary schools it was 22. In 2000, the average class size for secondary schools in China was 17. In primary schools the figure was 24.

However, the actual number of teachers in both primary and secondary sectors increased between 1990 and 2000. In 1990, there were 3·5 million secondary teachers and 5·6 million primary teachers. By 2000, this had increased to 4·3 million secondary teachers and 5·8 million in primary schools.

The changing pupil-teacher ratio must be explained by increasing numbers of children attending school. This is mainly because more youngsters are enrolling in schools and staying on longer. The effect of the One Child Policy has also been less than the government expected.

Number of Schools in China (2000)

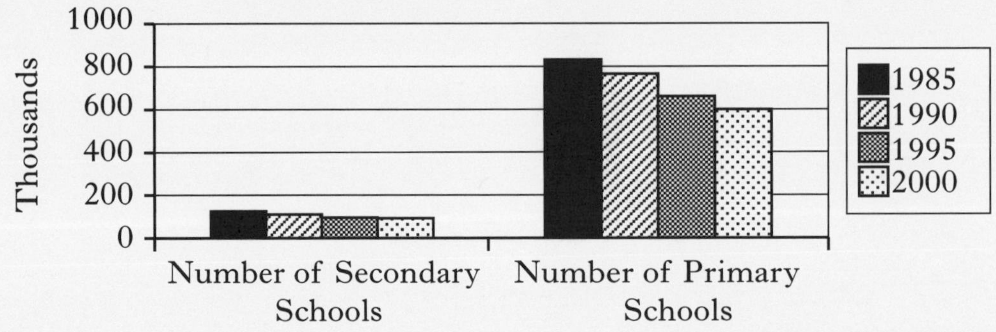

Selected Education Statistics for Provinces of Southern China (2000)

Province	Proportion of China's Population (%)	Proportion of University Graduates (%)
a Guizhou	2·9	1·2
b Guangxi	3·7	2·2
c Hunan	5·2	4·5
d Guangdong	5·6	5·9
e Fujian	2·7	2·6
f Jiangxi	3·3	2·8

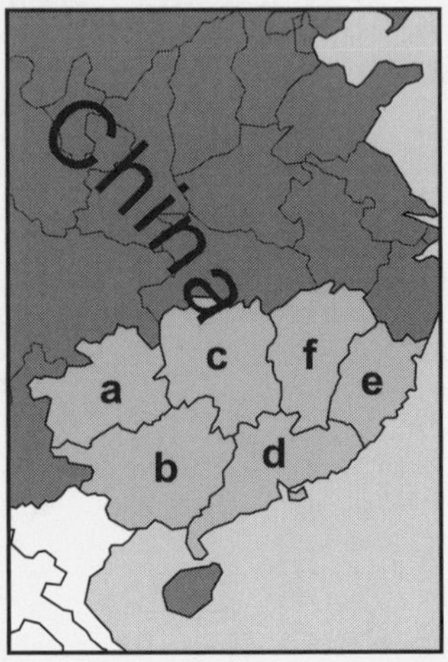

QUESTION 3 (C) (*b*) (CONTINUED)

Education statistics in China show a steady improvement. Educational achievement in Southern China is particularly good.

View of Jiang Zhi

Using **only** the information on page *sixteen*, explain **the extent to which** Jiang Zhi could be accused of being **selective in the use of facts.**

(Enquiry Skills, **6** marks)

[Turn over

QUESTION 3 (C) (CONTINUED)

(*c*) Study the information below then answer the question which follows.

Information about Crime in Hong Kong

Reported Crimes by Type of Offence			
	1996	**2000**	**2001**
Violent Crime	15 191	14 812	13 551
Non-violent crime	63 859	62 433	59 457
Total	79 050	77 245	73 008
Overall crime rate (per 100 000 population)	1228	1159	1086
Violent crime rate (per 100 000 population)	236	222	202
Persons arrested by Type of Offence			
	1996	**2000**	**2001**
Violent Crime	9910	9497	8435
Non-violent crime	37 247	31 433	30 394
Total	47 157	40 930	38 829
Rate of persons arrested for crime (per 100 000 population)	798	659	617

Using **only** the information above, what **conclusions** can be reached about crime in Hong Kong?

You **must** reach **one** conclusion about each of the following:

- detection rates for different types of crime (proportions of crime for which arrests are made)
- changes in crime statistics since 1996.

(Enquiry Skills, **4** marks)

NOW GO TO QUESTION 4 ON PAGE NINETEEN

SYLLABUS AREA 4—INTERNATIONAL RELATIONS

QUESTION 4

(*a*) *European countries have taken security measures to protect themselves against threats such as international terrorism.*

Describe, **in detail**, some of the *security measures taken by European countries to protect themselves against threats such as international terrorism.*

(Knowledge and Understanding, **4** marks)

(*b*) *Countries joining the European Union (EU) recently have done so for economic reasons.*

Explain, **in detail**, the *economic reasons for countries joining the European Union (EU).*

(Knowledge and Understanding, **4** marks)

[Turn over

QUESTION 4 (CONTINUED)

(*c*) Study sources 1, 2 and 3 below and opposite, then answer the question which follows.

Aims of the International Criminal Tribunal for the former Yugoslavia (ICTY)

The ICTY was established by the UN Security Council in 1993. Its main aims are:

1. to bring to justice the people mainly responsible for crimes against humanity, including genocide;
2. to try to stop further war crimes by showing the world that individuals will be prosecuted;
3. to help restore peace by promoting good relations between former enemies;
4. to be even-handed and deal equally with war crimes committed by all sides.

SOURCE 1

Selected factual Information on the ICTY (2002)

- Slobodan Milosevic, former President of the Federal Republic of Yugoslavia, was the most high profile detainee. He was charged with crimes against humanity including deportation, murder and persecution of thousands of people from Kosovo.
- Most of the other detainees were low ranking military personnel charged with carrying out killings under the orders of more senior officials.
- Most sentences handed out by the court have been between 2 years to 10 years imprisonment. However, one person got 25 years and another got 40 years.

What happened to the people who have been detained by the ICTY?

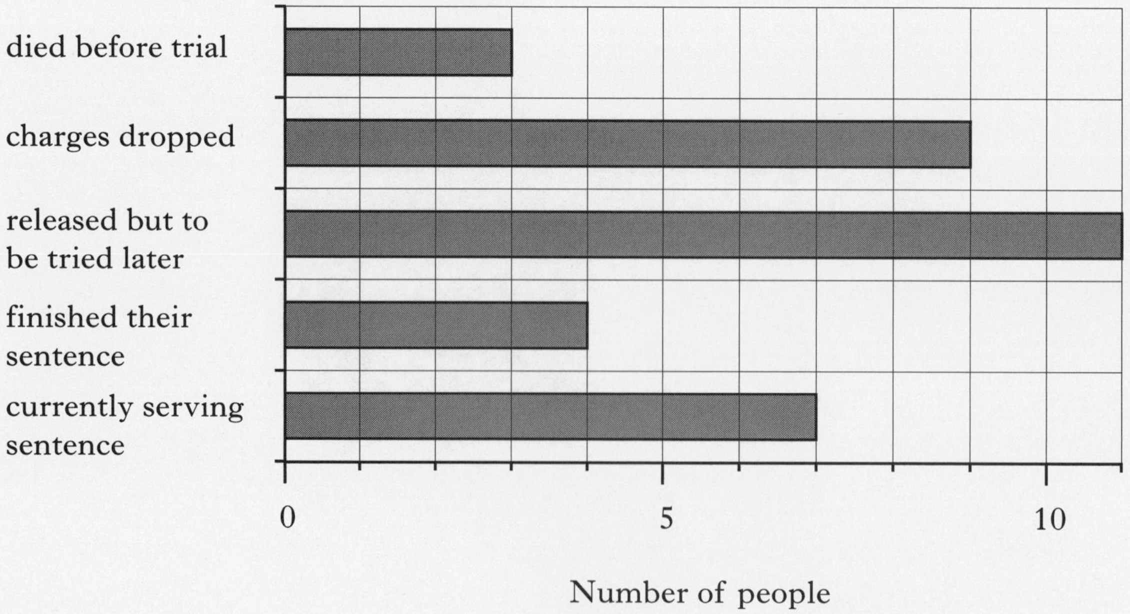

QUESTION 4 (*c*) (CONTINUED)

SOURCE 2

NATO WAR CRIMES IN YUGOSLAVIA

Milosevic and other Serbs are on trial for crimes against humanity, genocide and war crimes. However, Serbian people remember the crimes committed by NATO during its illegal campaign against Yugoslavia in 1999. NATO bombs, sanctioned by the UN, killed more than 500 Serbian civilians.

The ICTY must be independent in its pursuit of war criminals. The vast majority of people detained so far are Serbians. No-one working for the UN or NATO has been charged. It must investigate the political and military leadership of NATO including Bill Clinton and Tony Blair. Only then will the people of Serbia feel that real justice has been handed out and peace can return to the country.

Adapted from *Pravda on-line*

SOURCE 3

FRESH EVIDENCE OF WAR CRIMES IN YUGOSLAVIA

When the Serbians were forced to withdraw from Muslim areas of Bosnia, the evidence of war crimes was there for all to see. They had embarked on a policy of "ethnic cleansing" aimed at forcing the Muslim population out of certain towns and areas. The worst massacre was the one at Srebrenica in 1995 where approximately eight thousand Muslim males simply "disappeared". By 2002, the commander of the Serb forces responsible had not been arrested. In total, thousands of Serbians took part in war crimes.

More recently, the arrival of UN and NATO forces in Kosovo has uncovered more evidence of war crimes. Once again, the Serbians had tried a policy of ethnic cleansing — this time aimed against Albanians in the Kosovo region. The Serbian government had released criminals from jails in Belgrade on condition that they join para-military death squads. Thousands of Albanians were killed in Kosovo.

Many Serbians, the group who started the conflict, still support extreme political groups. There are no plans to withdraw UN and NATO peacekeepers from the former Yugoslavia at present — the situation remains very tense. The small number of prosecutions by the ICTY leaves the people of Kosovo worried about the future.

Adapted from *Kosovo watch* web site

The International Criminal Tribunal for the Former Yugoslavia (ICTY) has met each of its aims.

View of Tomas Moller

Using **only** information about the aims of the ICTY and Sources 1–3 above and opposite, give **detailed** reasons **for** and **against** the view of Tomas Moller.

(Enquiry Skills, **8** marks)

(*d*) Overall, do you **agree** with Tomas Moller? **Explain** why you have reached this decision.

(Enquiry Skills, **2** marks)

[*END OF QUESTION PAPER*]

[BLANK PAGE]

[BLANK PAGE]

G

2640/402

NATIONAL QUALIFICATIONS 2005

MONDAY, 23 MAY
10.20 AM–11.50 AM

MODERN STUDIES
STANDARD GRADE
General Level

1 Read every question carefully.

2 Answer all questions as fully as you can.

3 If you cannot do a question, go on to the next one. Try again later.

4 In question 3, answer **one** section only; Section (A) The USA **or** Section (B) Russia **or** Section (C) China.

5 Write your answers in the answer book provided. Indicate clearly, in the left hand margin, the question and section of question being answered. Do not write in the right hand margin.

SCOTTISH QUALIFICATIONS AUTHORITY

SYLLABUS AREA 1—LIVING IN A DEMOCRACY

QUESTION 1

(*a*) *Pressure groups can take different actions to try to influence the Government.*

Describe **two** actions which *pressure groups can take to try to influence the Government*.

(Knowledge & Understanding, **4** marks)

(*b*) Study the information below, then answer the question which follows.

Survey of People who did not Vote in the Scottish Parliament Election (2003)

Question 1: Why did you not vote?

	Percentage Agreeing
I meant to vote but circumstances prevented me	45
The parties are all the same	37
The Scottish Parliament cannot do very much	35
I am not interested	36
Obvious who would win so no point in voting	21

Question 2: Which new voting method would make you more likely to vote?

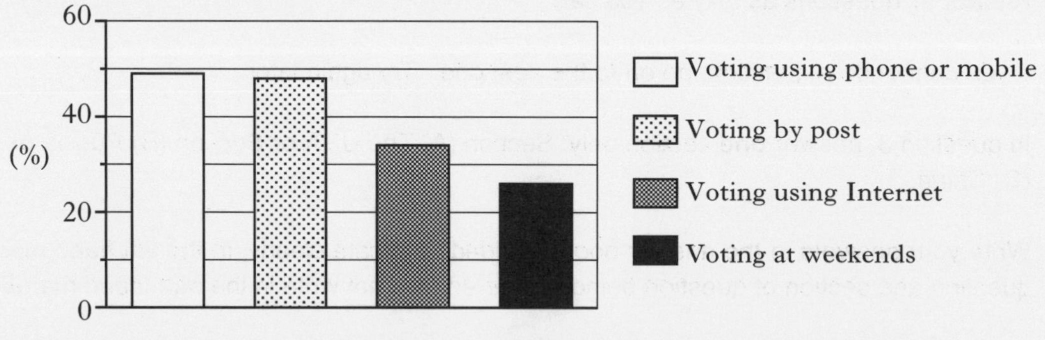

Statements by Meena Patel about people who do not vote

- Almost everyone says that the parties are all the same.
- Nearly half of the people would have voted but circumstances prevented them.
- Using the Internet would be the most likely way to increase voting.
- More people would vote if they could use their phone or mobile.

Using **only** the information above, write down **two** statements made by Meena Patel which are **exaggerated**.

Using the information, give **one** reason why **each** of the statements you have chosen is **exaggerated**.

(Enquiry Skills, **4** marks)

QUESTION 1 (CONTINUED)

You are investigating the topic in the box below.

The work of a Local Councillor

Answer questions (*c*), (*d*) and (*e*) which follow.

(*c*) As part of the **Planning Stage**, give **two** relevant **aims** for your investigation.

(Enquiry Skills, **2** marks)

You see the following advertisement in the local paper.

Study the advertisement carefully, then answer the question which follows.

Mary Millar, Inverdee Councillor
Answering Your Questions / Solving Your Problems

Surgeries will be held as follows:

Inverdee Town Hall

7.00 – 9.00 pm, first and third Tuesday each month
(No appointment required)

Inverdee Secondary School

7.00 – 9.00 pm, second and fourth Tuesday each month
(No appointment required)

Contact Mary Millar
Inverdee City Council Offices
Inverbrig Road
Inverdee
Phone: Inverdee 207086
e-mail: mmillar@inverdeecouncil.gov.uk

(*d*) You have decided to try and contact a local councillor to help you in your investigation.

From the advertisement above, choose **two** ways in which you could contact a local councillor.

For **each** way you have chosen, explain why it is a **good** way to get information to help in your investigation.

(Enquiry Skills, **4** marks)

(*e*) You also decide to use copies of your local newspaper from the past two years to help with your investigation.

Give **one** advantage and **one** disadvantage of using **past copies of the local newspaper** for your investigation.

(Enquiry Skills, **2** marks)

SYLLABUS AREA 2—CHANGING SOCIETY

QUESTION 2

(*a*) *The Government has tried to reduce poverty amongst families.*

Describe **two** recent Government policies which try *to reduce poverty amongst families.*

(Knowledge & Understanding, **4** marks)

(*b*) *Some elderly people can afford housing that is ideal for their needs.*

Give **two** reasons why *some elderly people can afford housing that is ideal for their needs.*

(Knowledge & Understanding, **4** marks)

(*c*) Study the information below, then answer the question which follows.

Survey of Employed People
The way in which you found out about your current job (%)

	Male	*Female*
Hearing from someone who works there	31	25
Replying to advertisement in newspaper	24	33
Making direct contact with employer	14	16
Through a private employment agency	11	9
By visiting the Job Centre	9	7
Some other way	11	10

Few people find out about their job through the Job Centre. Responding to advertisements in newspapers is the most common way of finding out about a job for both men and women.

View of David Reid

Using **only** the information above, give **one** reason to **support** and **one** reason to **oppose** the view of David Reid.

(Enquiry Skills, **4** marks)

QUESTION 2 (CONTINUED)

(*d*) Study the information below, then answer the question which follows.

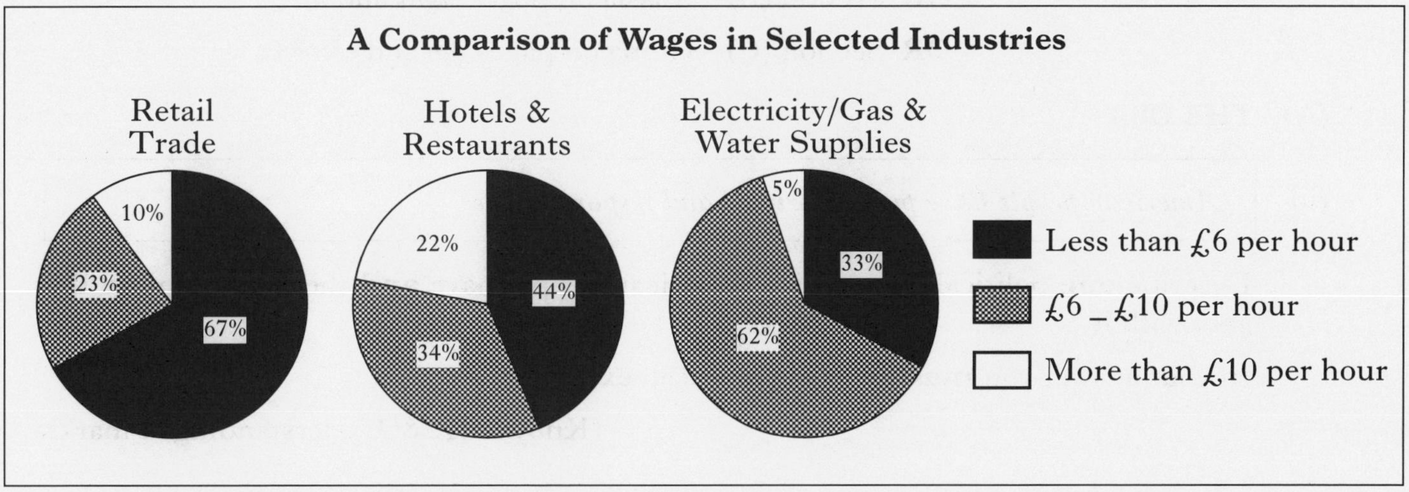

Write down **two** conclusions that can be reached about differences in wages between the selected industries.

You **must** only use the information above.

(Enquiry Skills, **4** marks)

[Turn over

SYLLABUS AREA 3—IDEOLOGIES

QUESTION 3

Answer **ONE** section only: Section (A)—The USA on pages *six* and *seven*

OR Section (B)—Russia on pages *eight* and *nine*

OR Section (C)—China on pages *ten* and *eleven*

(A) **THE USA**

(*a*) *American people have political rights and responsibilities.*

Describe **one** political right which American people have **and** the responsibility that goes with it.

In your answer you **must** refer to American examples.

(Knowledge & Understanding, **4** marks)

(*b*) *Many American people have started up their own businesses.*

Give **two** reasons why *many American people have started up their own businesses.*

In your answer you **must** refer to American examples.

(Knowledge & Understanding, **4** marks)

(*c*) Study the information below, then answer the question which follows.

USA—Student Dentists by Ethnic Group

Ethnic Group	***1992***	***2002***
White	11,185	11,176
African American	940	808
Hispanic	1,254	912
Asian	2,519	4,317
Native American	53	99

Statements from a speech by George Plant

- The number of White students has gone down by a large amount.
- Numbers of both Asian and Native American students have increased significantly.
- In 2002, there were more White students than all other groups put together.
- The biggest decline in student dentists has been for African Americans.

Using **only** the information above, write down **two** statements made by George Plant which are **exaggerated**.

Using the information, give **one** reason why **each** of the statements you have chosen is **exaggerated**.

(Enquiry Skills, **4** marks)

QUESTION 3 (A) (CONTINUED)

(*d*) Study Sources 1 and 2 below, then answer the question which follows.

SOURCE 1

Extract from an Election Speech by Democratic Party Candidate, November 2004

In this election, Americans must make important decisions about the direction our country should take. For example, some people cannot afford health care insurance. We must expand Government schemes such as Medicare to help them.

This may mean an increase in tax. However, I think most people will accept this increase if it is used to improve public services such as health and education. It is important that everyone votes to make sure that their views are put forward.

SOURCE 2

Extract from an Election Speech by a Republican Party Candidate, November 2004

Our nation is the richest in the world because of our free market economy. People who work hard want to be allowed to keep their money and not have it taken away from them by the Government in higher taxes.

The Government has got many things to spend its money on. The best way of achieving good health care for all is by encouraging private medical insurance. If you vote for me, I'll make sure the job is done.

Sources 1 and 2 give information about **the different policies of candidates at the 2004 American elections**.

Write down **two** of the **differences** between the policies of these candidates.

You **must** only use information from the Sources above.

(Enquiry Skills, **4** marks)

NOW GO TO QUESTION 4 ON PAGE TWELVE

QUESTION 3 (CONTINUED)

(B) **RUSSIA**

(*a*) *Russian people have political rights and responsibilities.*

Describe **one** political right which Russian people have **and** the responsibility that goes with it.

In your answer you **must** refer to Russian examples.

(Knowledge & Understanding, **4** marks)

(*b*) *The Russian Government has encouraged people to start up their own businesses.*

Give **two** reasons why *the Russian Government has encouraged people to start up their own businesses.*

In your answer you **must** refer to Russian examples.

(Knowledge & Understanding, **4** marks)

(*c*) Study the information below, then answer the question which follows.

Russia—Selected Health Statistics

	2000	***2001***
Number of doctors (thousands)	683	682
Number of nurses (thousands)	1,612	1,564
Number of hospitals (thousands)	11	10
Number of health centres (thousands)	21	21

Statements from a speech by Alexander Dassaev

- The number of doctors in Russia has gone down by a large amount.
- The number of both doctors and nurses has gone down.
- The total number of hospitals and health centres in Russia was less in 2000 than in 2001.
- As the number of doctors and nurses has fallen, so has the number of hospitals.

Using **only** the information above, write down **two** statements made by Alexander Dassaev which are **exaggerated**.

Using the information, give **one** reason why **each** of the statements you have chosen is **exaggerated**.

(Enquiry Skills, **4** marks)

QUESTION 3 (B) (CONTINUED)

(*d*) Study Sources 1 and 2 below, then answer the question which follows.

SOURCE 1

Extract from an Election Speech by a Yabloko Candidate, December 2003

The Government needs to spend more time on improving health and education services. These are the most important issues for the voters.

We believe that the richest people in Russia should pay very high taxes on their incomes. However, people who made money back in the 1990s should not now have it taken away from them. They took big risks to help the Russian economy change from the Communist system to a Capitalist system.

SOURCE 2

Extract from an Election Speech by a Communist Party Candidate, December 2003

Taxes should be changed so that the very wealthy pay more. The gap between rich and poor in Russia is too great. People who made huge sums of money in the late 1990s should be made to pay back most of it to the Government.

The biggest issue at this election is Russia's foreign policy. Our country should not be making such strong links with the European Union and the USA.

Sources 1 and 2 give information about **the different policies of candidates at the 2003 Russian elections**.

Write down **two** of the **differences** between the policies of these candidates.

You **must** only use information from the Sources above.

(Enquiry Skills, **4** marks)

NOW GO TO QUESTION 4 ON PAGE TWELVE

QUESTION 3 (CONTINUED)

(C) **CHINA**

(*a*) *Chinese people have limited political rights.*

Describe **one** political right which Chinese people have.

Describe **one further** political right which many Chinese people would like to be given.

In your answer you **must** refer to Chinese examples.

(Knowledge & Understanding, **4** marks)

(*b*) *The Chinese Government has encouraged people to start up their own businesses.*

Give **two** reasons why *the Chinese Government has encouraged people to start up their own businesses.*

In your answer you **must** refer to Chinese examples.

(Knowledge & Understanding, **4** marks)

(*c*) Study the information below, then answer the question which follows.

China—Selected Health Statistics

	1999	***2000***
Number of hospitals and clinics (thousands)	309	320
Number of doctors (thousands)	1,303	1,300
Number of nurses (thousands)	1,007	1,005
Official number of drug addicts (thousands)	572	681

Statements from a speech by Lee Quangxing

- The number of doctors in China has gone down by a large amount.
- The total number of nurses and doctors in China has gone down.
- The number of drug addicts went up by more than 100,000 between 1999 and 2000.
- The number of drug addicts in China has gone up while the numbers of hospitals and clinics has gone down.

Using **only** the information above, write down **two** statements made by Lee Quangxing which are **exaggerated**.

Using the information, give **one** reason why **each** of the statements you have chosen is **exaggerated**.

(Enquiry Skills, **4** marks)

QUESTION 3 (C) (CONTINUED)

(*d*) Study Sources 1 and 2 below, then answer the question which follows.

SOURCE 1

Extract from a Communist Party speech about Hong Kong

Elections were held in Hong Kong recently. All people had the opportunity to vote in a fair election. We need to have strong links with the Communist Party in China and to make similar laws. This will make our country stronger.

The Communist Party knows that Hong Kong must keep its special economic status. The Government needs to work with large businesses in Hong Kong to create more jobs. This is the biggest problem for the Government.

SOURCE 2

Extract from a Non-Communist Party (Dissident) speech about Hong Kong

The most important issue facing the Government in Hong Kong is how to create new jobs. Many jobs have been lost in recent years. Hong Kong must have the freedom to make economic decisions which are different from those in China. Hong Kong must keep its special economic status. This will be of great benefit.

The recent elections in Hong Kong were not free and fair. Hong Kong should be able to decide on its own laws and not have to follow the Communist Party in China.

Sources 1 and 2 give information about **the different policies of parties towards Hong Kong**.

Write down **two** of the **differences** between the policies of these parties.

You **must** only use information from the Sources above.

(Enquiry Skills, **4** marks)

NOW GO TO QUESTION 4 ON PAGE TWELVE

SYLLABUS AREA 4—INTERNATIONAL RELATIONS

QUESTION 4

(*a*) *European countries such as the UK have been involved in international conflicts in recent years.*

Describe **two** ways in which *European countries such as the UK have been involved in international conflicts in recent years.*

In your answer, refer to examples that you have studied.

(Knowledge & Understanding, **4** marks)

(*b*) *Many countries have joined the European Union recently.*

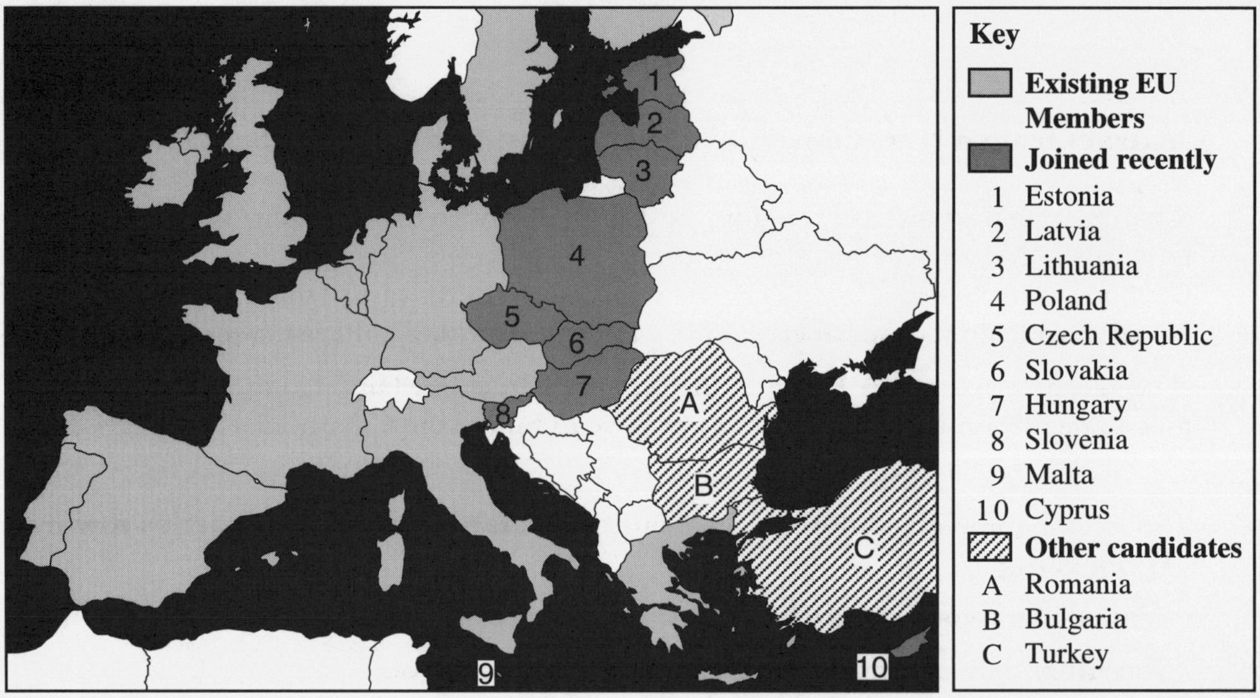

Give **two** reasons to explain why *many countries have joined the European Union recently*.

(Knowledge & Understanding, **4** marks)

QUESTION 4 (CONTINUED)

(*c*) Study Sources 1 and 2 below, then answer the question which follows.

SOURCE 1

Result of Swedish Referendum on joining the Single European Currency (Euro), 2003

Do you think Sweden should join the Euro?

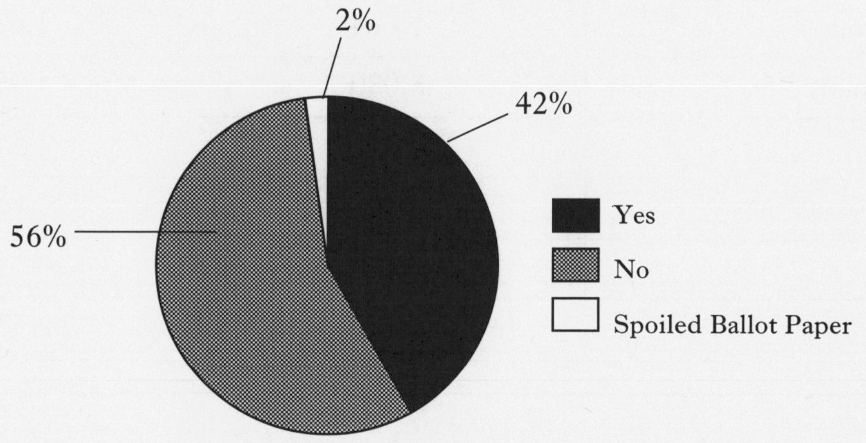

SOURCE 2

Newsfile, September 2003

Sweden has voted on the Single European Currency (Euro). There are currently 15 members of the EU and 12 of them belong to the Eurozone. Many Swedish businesses feel that they will lose trade because Sweden will not become part of the Eurozone and they may seek compensation from the Government. There will not be another referendum for 10 years.

The Swedish referendum did not produce a clear result. Swedish businesses were delighted with this result.

View of Katie Halfpenny, Economist

Using only Sources 1 and 2, give **two** reasons to **disagree** with the view of Katie Halfpenny.

(Enquiry Skills, **4** marks)

[Turn over for question 4(*d*) on Page *fourteen*

QUESTION 4 (CONTINUED)

(*d*) Study the information below, then answer the question which follows.

Aid donated by Selected Countries, 2000 and 2001 (in US million dollars)

Donor Country	*2000*	*2001*
Austria	423	533
Denmark	1,664	1,634
Germany	5,030	4,990
Japan	13,508	9,847
New Zealand	113	112
UK	4,501	4,579
USA	9,955	11,429

Write down **two** conclusions about the **changes** in aid donated by selected countries.

You should write **one** conclusion about **each** of the following.

- The country giving most aid in 2001 compared to 2000
- The changes in the amount of aid given by different countries

You **must** only use the information above.

(Enquiry Skills, **4** marks)

[*END OF QUESTION PAPER*]

C

2640/403

NATIONAL QUALIFICATIONS 2005

MONDAY, 23 MAY
1.00 PM – 3.00 PM

MODERN STUDIES
STANDARD GRADE
Credit Level

1 Read every question carefully.

2 Answer all questions as fully as you can.

3 If you cannot do a question, go on to the next one. Try again later.

4 In question 3, answer **one** section only: Section (A) The USA **or** Section (B) Russia **or** Section (C) China.

5 Write your answers in the answer book provided. Indicate clearly, in the left hand margin, the question and section of question being answered. Do not write in the right hand margin.

SCOTTISH QUALIFICATIONS AUTHORITY

THB 2640/403 6/3/14670

[BLANK PAGE]

SYLLABUS AREA 1—LIVING IN A DEMOCRACY

QUESTION 1

(*a*) *Our elected representatives work on behalf of people in many different ways.*

Choose **either** Local Councillors **or** MSPs **or** MPs.

Describe, **in detail**, the ways in which the type of representative you have chosen works on behalf of the people they represent.

(Knowledge & Understanding, **6** marks)

(*b*) Study the information below, then answer the question which follows.

Proportion of workers who are trade union members (Great Britain 1990–2000)

	1990	1995	2000
Number of union members (thousands)	8835	7309	7321
All employment	33·9%	28·8%	27%
Gender			
Male	44%	35%	30%
Female	32%	30%	29%
Type of work			
Manual	42%	33%	28%
Non-manual	35%	32%	30%
Full- or part-time work			
Full-time	43%	36%	33%
Part-time	22%	21%	23%
Employment Sector			
Manufacturing	44%	34%	28%
Services	37%	33%	31%

Trade unions have become more gender equal since 1990. Unions are now strongest in manual work and the manufacturing sector despite recent changes in British industry.

View of Frances Naismith

Using **only** the information above, give **one** reason to **support** and **one** reason to **oppose** the view of Frances Naismith.

(Enquiry Skills, **4** marks)

QUESTION 1 (CONTINUED)

(*c*) Study Sources 1, 2 and 3 below and opposite, then answer the question which follows.

SOURCE 1

The UK Population	
Age profile (% of the age group 20–59)	**2001**
20–29	23·7
30–39	29·5
40–49	24·4
50–59	22·4
Total	**100%**
Educational Background	**2001**
School only	79·4
FE College	7·2
University	13·4
Total	**100%**
Occupational Background	**2001**
Manual workers	52·3
Financial and business	19·0
Public administration, defence, legal, political	5·4
Education, social work, health	18·3
Other	5·0
Total	**100%**
Gender and Ethnic minority background	
The UK population is 49% male and 51% female. The UK population is 94·5% white and 5·5% from ethnic minority backgrounds. In Scotland 96·5% are from white and 3·5% from ethnic minority backgrounds.	

SOURCE 2

Westminster Parliament	
Age profile (MPs) (% of the age group 20–59)	**2001**
20–29	0·7
30–39	14·1
40–49	41·6
50–59	43·6
Total	**100%**
Educational Background (MPs)	**2001**
School only	8·7
FE College	16·5
University	74·8
Total	**100%**
Occupational Background (MPs)	**2001**
Manual workers	20·4
Financial and business	23·4
Public administration, defence, legal, political	36·6
Education, social work, health	17·6
Other	2·0
Total	**100%**
Gender and Ethnic minority background	
In Westminster 17·9% of the MPs are female and 2% from an ethnic minority background which many people feel is not good enough.	

QUESTION 1(*c*) (CONTINUED)

SOURCE 3

Scottish Parliament

Age profile of MSPs (% of the age group 20–59)	**1999**	**2003**
20–29	4·2	1·0
30–39	27·7	18·6
40–49	40·3	41·6
50–59	27·8	38·8
Total	**100%**	**100%**
Educational Background of MSPs	**1999**	**2003**
School only	8·1	8·6
FE College	18·5	15·5
University	73·4	75·9
Total	**100%**	**100%**
Occupational Background of MSPs	**1999**	**2003**
Manual workers	10·9	7·7
Financial and business	20·3	22·9
Public administration, defence, legal, political	27·4	22·5
Education, social work, health	28·1	33·6
Other	13·3	13·3
Total	**100%**	**100%**

Gender and Ethnic minority background

In the areas of gender and ethnic minority equality, the Scottish Parliament hoped that it would improve representation. The Scottish Parliament in 1999 was 63% male whilst in 2003 it was 60·5% male. Scottish Parliament MSPs were 100% white in both 1999 and 2003.

It was hoped that one of the successes of the Scottish Parliament, when comparing it to the Westminster Parliament, would be in achieving fairer representation for all groups.

Using **only** the information in Sources 1, 2 and 3 above and opposite, what conclusions can be reached about **the success of the Scottish Parliament, when comparing it to the Westminster Parliament, in achieving fairer representation for all groups**?

You must reach conclusions about **four** of the following headings. For **each** conclusion, you must refer in each case to Sources 1, 2 and 3.

- Women
- People from an ethnic minority background
- People under 40
- People without further and higher education qualifications
- Manual workers

(Enquiry Skills, **8** marks)

[BLANK PAGE]

SYLLABUS AREA 2—CHANGING SOCIETY

QUESTION 2

(*a*) *Getting a job is a challenge for young people. Many young people need help which is available from Central Government, local Councils and voluntary organisations.*

Describe **two** different ways in which **either** Central Government **or** local Councils **or** voluntary organisations help young people to get a job.

For **each** way, explain why it might be effective in helping a young person get a job.

(Knowledge and Understanding, **6** marks)

(*b*) *Some people prefer to work from home for a variety of reasons. Technology allows them to do this.*

Explain, **in detail**, the reasons why *some people prefer to work from home.*

In answering this question you **must** refer to:

- the needs of some people
- the technology available.

(Knowledge and Understanding, **4** marks)

[Turn over

QUESTION 2 (CONTINUED)

(*c*) Study Sources 1, 2 and 3 below and opposite, then answer the question which follows.

SOURCE 1

Population of Scotland in 2000 (Selected Age Ranges)

	Number (000s)	% of total pop
45 – 64	1212	23·7
65 – 74	440	8·6
75+	347	6·8
Total population	5115	100

SOURCE 2

TABLE 1

Annual numbers of consultations with primary care health workers in Scotland in 2000 (figures in thousands)

	Age 45–54	Age 55–64	Age 65+
Doctor	2272	1967	3769
Practice Nurse	783	784	1600
Health Visitor	30	40	288
District Nurse	231	275	1989

TABLE 2

Day patient and inpatient admission rates; by age group: Scotland 2000

	Annual rates per 1000 population		
	Day Patients	Inpatients (more than 1 day)	
		Planned Admissions	Emergency Admissions
Males			
45–54	83	40	80
55–64	133	77	124
65–74	184	118	194
75–84	206	143	322
85+	170	137	498
Females			
45–54	101	51	62
55–64	129	69	86
65–74	146	87	145
75–84	136	94	155
85+	98	90	427

QUESTION 2(*c*) (CONTINUED)

SOURCE 3

Simply the best or not?

Comments from some over 65s on their experiences of the National Health Service (NHS) in Scotland.

- My wife has had a lot of treatment on the NHS. The NHS has been wonderful for us.

  Harold, 75

- There was no effort to ensure that I had adequate back-up at home after I left the hospital.

  Elsie, 73

- It's hard to get a doctor as you've far too long to wait for an appointment.

  George, 73

- The emergency treatment was excellent. Rushed to hospital within ten minutes and seen by a doctor within another two or three minutes.

  Mildred, 68

What over 65s think of health care services in Scotland (2003)

	In need of a lot of Improvement %	In need of some Improvement %	Satisfactory %	Very Good %
Quality of medical treatment in hospitals	12	39	41	8
Quality of nursing care in hospitals	12	30	37	21
General condition of hospital buildings	18	39	36	7
Quality of medical treatment by your local doctor	7	23	51	19

The elderly are the biggest users of the NHS in Scotland and they are satisfied with the quality of health care they receive.

View of Norman Macphail

Using **only** Sources 1, 2 and 3, explain **the extent to which** Norman Macphail could be accused of being **selective in the use of facts**.

(Enquiry Skills, **8** marks)

[BLANK PAGE]

SYLLABUS AREA 3—IDEOLOGIES

QUESTION 3

Answer **one** section only: Section (A)—The USA on pages *eleven* to *thirteen*
OR Section (B)—Russia on pages *fifteen* to *seventeen*
OR Section (C)—China on pages *nineteen* to *twenty-one*

(A) **THE USA**

(*a*) *There continues to be social and economic inequality in the USA.*

Explain, **in detail**, why there is ***social and economic inequality*** *in the USA.*

In your answer you **must** use American examples.

(Knowledge and Understanding, **8** marks)

[Turn over

QUESTION 3 (A) (CONTINUED)

(*b*) Study the information about Rockford City below. Also study the information in Sources 1 and 2 opposite. Sources 1 and 2 contain information about the two people who are candidates to become Mayor of Rockford City.

Information about Rockford City

- Rockford City is a small city of about 21 000 people. It is situated in the Eastern USA, about an hour's drive away from Raleigh, the state capital. It is a wealthy community with incomes well above the national average. However, there are a number of issues which concern local people.
- The proposed new Red Pine commercial project will provide a range of shopping, recreation and dining opportunities. Most local people believe that this will help economic growth, attracting shoppers from other towns. However, at present the site is an attractive wood used by local people for leisure.
- There are over 7000 students attending the 5 Elementary, 3 Middle and 2 High schools in Rockford City. The standard of education is good but Rockford High school is old and in poor condition. It is due to be rebuilt and most residents want to see it being turned into a magnet school which will promote racial diversity and offer better course options.
- Public transport is poor and most people make extensive use of their cars. However, the condition of many roads has been criticised—especially in housing areas where there are many potholes causing damage to cars. There have also been calls to improve the main road to the state capital to help commuters and attract new jobs to the city.
- In 2003, Hurricane Isobel caused serious flooding in the area. As a result many homes and businesses were damaged and it is estimated that it will cost over $200 million to put right. Improvements to the storm water drainage system would help reduce this risk in the future.

Opinion poll

Which of these is the most important problem facing Rockford City at present?	
Environment	21%
Poor schools	26%
Flood defences	26%
Public transport	10%
Local economy/jobs	17%

Selected Economic Statistics for Rockford City

	2000	**2003**
Average earnings	$25 750	$26 906
Unemployment	10%	7%
Average house price	$95 000	$110 000

Did you vote at the last mayoral elections?

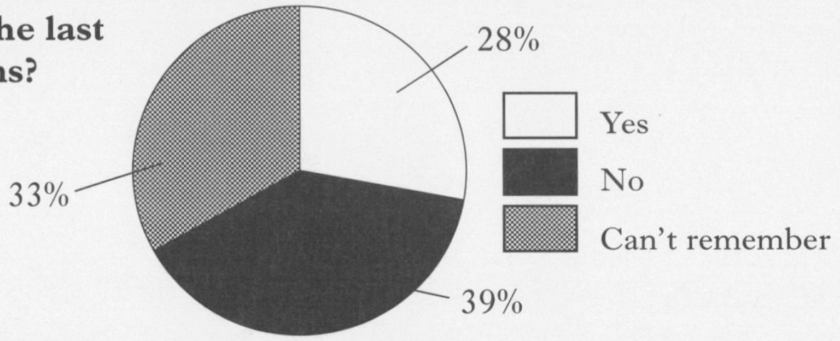

QUESTION 3 (A) (*b*) (CONTINUED)

SOURCE 1

Profile of Brent Landon

Brent Landon has been mayor of Rockford City for the past 4 years. He qualified as a lawyer over 20 years ago, and has worked in the city ever since. As a result, he knows the community well and has used his legal knowledge to assist local charities.

Extracts from his campaign website:

- My first priority is the local economy. During my term in office, there have been more jobs created and higher pay. I want this to continue but not by building a new shopping complex. The city needs parks and open spaces where people can enjoy their leisure time.
- We can be proud of our local schools. However, I want only the best for our children and I will strive to make the changes to the education system that are necessary to bring children from all racial backgrounds together.
- The recent floods took us all by surprise. I will ensure that this city invests in flood prevention schemes to minimise the effect of future events.
- I will make public transport a big priority.
- I will expand the Voter Registration Programme to get more people involved in local politics.

SOURCE 2

Profile of Louise Crossan

Louise Crossan is a businesswoman who owns several retail outlets employing 35 local people. She moved to Rockford City 5 years ago and, although she has not held public office, she is a member of the local Chamber of Commerce.

Extracts from her campaign website:

- I want to see our community growing. I will work to attract new retail and leisure businesses to the city. This will help our local economy to continue its economic growth.
- The city has been spending too much which has resulted in local property taxes having to be increased. This is bad for business. I will balance the books even if it means postponing less important projects such as a new flood defence scheme.
- The condition of our streets is very poor. Regular maintenance must be improved. I will work to ensure the completion of improved highways to our neighbouring towns and cities.
- Education is vital. We must improve some of our older schools. I am for the creation of a magnet school in Rockford City even though it will involve large numbers of children having to travel to school.
- There is no point wasting money on Voter Registration Schemes—democracy already works well in Rockford City.

Using **only** the information about Rockford City and Sources 1 and 2 above, **explain which person would be the most suitable to be elected by the people of Rockford City as their new Mayor.**

Give **detailed** reasons to **explain your choice** and **why you rejected the other candidate**.

In your answer you **must** relate information about the city to the information about the two candidates.

(Enquiry Skills, **10** marks)

[NOW GO TO QUESTION 4 ON PAGE 23]

[BLANK PAGE]

QUESTION 3 (CONTINUED)

(B) **RUSSIA**

(*a*)

Social and economic inequality has grown in Russia in recent years.

Explain, **in detail**, why ***social and economic inequality*** *has grown in Russia in recent years.*

In your answer you **must** use Russian examples.

(Knowledge and Understanding, **8** marks)

[Turn over

QUESTION 3 (B) (CONTINUED)

(*b*) Study the information about the city of Izhevsk below. Also study the information in Sources 1 and 2 opposite. Sources 1 and 2 contain information about the two people who are candidates to become leader of the local Council for Izhevsk.

Information about Izhevsk

Izhevsk is the largest city in Udmurtia. The city is located in the Ural mountains to the east of Moscow. The population of Izhevsk is 700 000. The city is typical of many in Russia.

- Izhevsk lake is a popular place with local people. It has an inland beach where people can sunbathe and enjoy the water. Concerns have been growing recently about pollution with several bathers reporting mystery illnesses after bathing in the lake. There is speculation that this may be linked to the local zinc-processing industry.
- Izhevsk is an important car and lorry manufacturing centre. Car ownership has increased in recent years but the quality of the road system is very poor. Deep potholes cause damage to vehicles and during the rush hour there are frequent traffic jams. Dangerous driving leads to many accidents.
- There are three large armaments factories in Izhevsk. These produce guns, ammunition and other military equipment. The Russian government has been buying fewer weapons recently and this has led to cut-backs in the factory order books. Unemployment has been rising as workers lose their jobs.
- The University of Izhevsk used to be regarded as one of the best in the country. The Faculty of Engineering had a particularly good reputation. Lack of funds means that many university staff have now been paid off and the facilities badly need upgraded.

Opinion poll	
Which of these is the most important problem facing Izhevsk at present?	
Rising crime	23%
Poor schools	18%
Poor health services	14%
Dealing with Chechnya	9%
Corrupt politicians	36%

Do you believe that the Russian government should continue with a space programme?

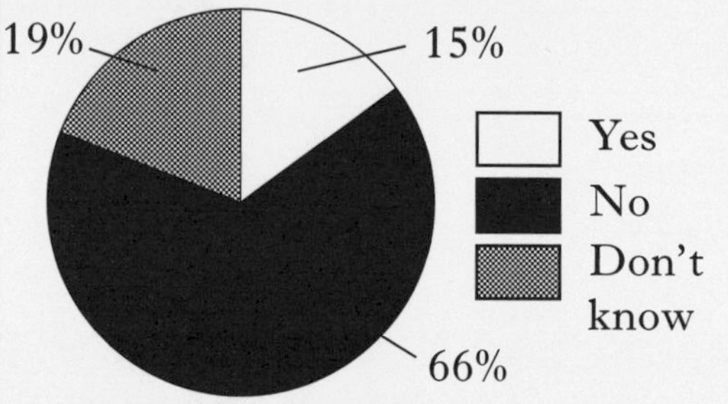

Did you vote at the last Council elections?

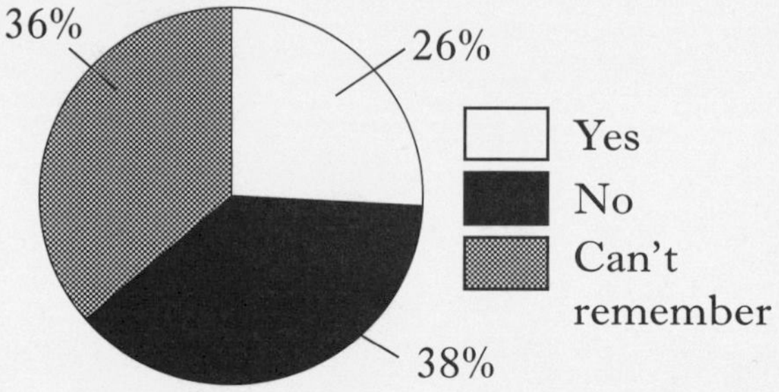

QUESTION 3 (B) (*b*) (CONTINUED)

SOURCE 1

Profile of Vasili Kharine

51-year-old Vasili was born in Izhevsk. However, he has worked in other towns and cities nearby in recent years. When he was younger he played football for the local team. He has been involved in local government in a neighbouring city.

Extracts from his campaign leaflet:

- I am keenly interested in environmental issues. As a student I got into trouble with the authorities for trying to promote the activities of "Greenpeace".
- In my present role as Director of roads and traffic management, I have succeeded in reducing traffic congestion which has led to a decrease in serious accidents.
- Poor health services are of great concern to the voters. Improving them is my top priority.
- Russia needs a higher profile around the world. For that reason, we must continue with the space programme. Russia should be in the forefront of modern technology and science.
- I think it is terrible that some people in Izhevsk are frightened to leave their homes at night because of crime. Violence and robbery are on the increase—I will take steps to deal with this.

SOURCE 2

Profile of Dmitri Kulkov

52-year-old Dmitri was born in Izhevsk and has lived there for most of his life. He had a spell in the Armed Forces, rising to the rank of Captain. He was decorated for his bravery during the Afghan War in 1979. He has no previous involvement in politics.

Extracts from his campaign leaflet:

- There is no evidence that the people of Izhevsk are bored with politics. The turnout at recent elections has been very good.
- I believe that the Russian government should expand its armed forces. I believe that Russia needs the weapons to be a strong force in an unstable world.
- The decline of the University of Izhevsk has been bad for the city. I promise that there will be fresh investment to bring the university up to modern standards.
- Money that has been spent on Russia's ambitious space programme should be diverted to internal military threats. I also think that instead of sending cosmonauts into space we would be better dealing with the Chechens and any other terrorist threats.
- Some politicians have let the people down badly through their links with crime. They have taken bribes. I will deal strongly with corruption in government.

Using **only** the information about Izhevsk and Sources 1 and 2 above, **explain which person would be the most suitable to be elected by the people of Izhevsk as their new local Council leader.**

Give **detailed** reasons to **explain your choice** and **why you rejected the other candidate**.

In your answer you **must** relate information about the city to the information about the two candidates.

(Enquiry Skills, **10** marks)

[NOW GO TO QUESTION 4 ON PAGE 23]

[BLANK PAGE]

QUESTION 3 (CONTINUED)

(C) **CHINA**

(*a*) | *Social and economic inequality has grown in China in recent years.* |

Explain, **in detail**, why ***social and economic inequality*** *has grown in China in recent years*.

In your answer you **must** use Chinese examples.

(Knowledge and Understanding, **8** marks)

[Turn over

QUESTION 3 (C) (CONTINUED)

(*b*) Study the information about the village of Sanbu below. Also study the information in Sources 1 and 2 opposite. Sources 1 and 2 contain information about the two people who are candidates to become head of the village Committee in Sanbu.

Information about Sanbu

Sanbu is a village in Central China. It is 30 miles from the nearest large town. It has a population of 19 000.

- Agriculture has been an important part of the economy of Sanbu. Many farmers have taken advantage of the changes in agricultural policy to expand their businesses and now want more access to the markets in nearby towns. To do this, they need better roads and transport facilities. Many resent previous spending on projects like a pig-raising project forced on them by a decision taken by the Communist Party in Beijing and want to make their own decisions on investment.

- The major industry in Sanbu is a factory which strips down parts from old American computers and mobile phones. This employs 120 people and the local Communist Party is keen to see this expand to stop the drift to the towns of young people seeking better employment opportunities. This factory releases toxic chemicals like mercury and dioxins into the air and water. There is suspicion that this is the cause of rising cancer cases in local school children.

- Drug addiction is a growing health problem in Sanbu. The village is on a new drug trail from central China to the cities in the south. Many of the younger villagers have become drug addicts. Their parents are desperate for more help for their children to combat the problem and also the threat of AIDS.

Opinion poll	
Which of these is the most important problem facing Sanbu at present?	
Poor access to markets	29%
Poor water supply	4%
Creating industrial jobs	26%
Poor health services	16%
Education	25%

Do you think that democracy should be extended in China?	
Yes	59%
No	34%
Don't know	7%

Do you agree with the Communist Party that drug addicts should be severely punished?

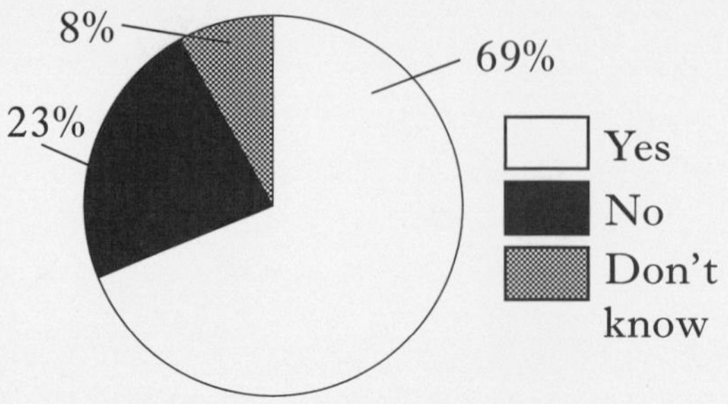

QUESTION 3 (C) (*b*) (CONTINUED)

SOURCE 1

Profile of Fang Zhizhen

Fang is 53 years old and has been a member of the Communist Party for 35 years. He is married with one son in accordance with the One Child Policy. He was educated locally and has only left the village for Party rallies. The local Communist Party has nominated Fang to continue in his post as head of the village Committee. Fang has been involved in local government for many years.

Extracts from his campaign poster:

- I support fully all the policies of the Communist Party and believe that few people in China want more democracy.
- I am proud that the Communist Party was responsible for bringing many computer jobs to the village and believe that the future economy of Sanbu lies in expanding industry.
- I am a firm believer in the Communist Party policy of a tough line on drugs. I believe that the only way to tackle the problem of drug addiction is to have tough penalties on users. The party is right to use severe punishments for this crime.
- One of my main aims for the future is to ensure that conditions for people in Sanbu improve. I have plans to improve the water and sewage as well as ensuring that the school is provided with more resources and a better building.

SOURCE 2

Profile of Qumo Aqu

Qumo was born in Beijing and educated at Beijing University. She spent a year in the USA studying medicine. After her marriage, she came to practise as a doctor in Sanbu. She has two children, one boy and one girl and is glad that the Communist Party has adopted a new policy of "One-Son-Two-Children". She is not a member of the Communist Party and believes that people should have a bigger choice in who runs their village Committee.

Extracts from her campaign poster:

- I believe that local farmers should be supported as more people depend on agriculture than industry. I am of the opinion that better roads would make it easier to get products to markets.
- I am opposed to industries like the computer industry which damage our environment and affect the health of our children.
- As a doctor, I see the effects of the drug problem but believe that addicts need help rather than punishment. Addicts need acupuncture and herbal medicine as well as counselling. This is a better way to deal with the problem.
- Money should be spent on education and improvements in the water supply. If people were able to decide for themselves what taxes should be spent on, this would ensure that the needs of the village were met and people would be more willing to pay.

Using **only** the information about Sanbu and Sources 1 and 2 above, **explain which person would be the most suitable to be elected by the people of Sanbu as their head of the village Committee.**

Give **detailed** reasons to **explain your choice** and **why you rejected the other candidate**.

In your answer you **must** relate information about the village to the information about the two candidates.

(Enquiry Skills, **10** marks)

[NOW GO TO QUESTION 4 ON PAGE 23]

[BLANK PAGE]

SYLLABUS AREA 4—INTERNATIONAL RELATIONS

QUESTION 4

(*a*) *Wealthy countries have had economic power over African countries in recent years.*

Describe, **in detail**, the ways in which wealthy countries from outside Africa have used their **economic power** in their relations with less well-off African countries in recent years.

(Knowledge and Understanding, **4** marks)

(*b*) *The aid policies of the United Nations have helped meet the needs of some African countries.*

Describe, **in detail**, the ways in which the *aid policies of the United Nations have helped meet the **needs** of some African countries.*

(Knowledge and Understanding, **4** marks)

[Turn over

QUESTION 4 (CONTINUED)

You have been asked to carry out **two** investigations.

The first investigation is on the topic in the box below.

The European Union (EU) in the 21st Century.

Now answer questions (*c*) and (*d*) which follow.

(*c*) State a relevant **hypothesis** for your investigation.

(Enquiry Skills, **2** marks)

(*d*) Give **two** relevant **aims** to help you prove or disprove your hypothesis.

(Enquiry Skills, **2** marks)

The second investigation is on the topic in the box below.

The North Atlantic Treaty Organisation (NATO) in the 21st Century.

Now answer questions (*e*) and (*f*) which follow.

Your class decides to carry out a survey of public opinion about NATO.

(*e*) Describe, **in detail**, **two** factors that must be taken into account when designing and carrying out a survey.

(Enquiry Skills, **4** marks)

QUESTION 4 (CONTINUED)

(*f*) You also decide to carry out a search on the Internet.

You enter the phrase, "NATO in the 21st Century", into the BBC news website search engine.

Six results are shown below.

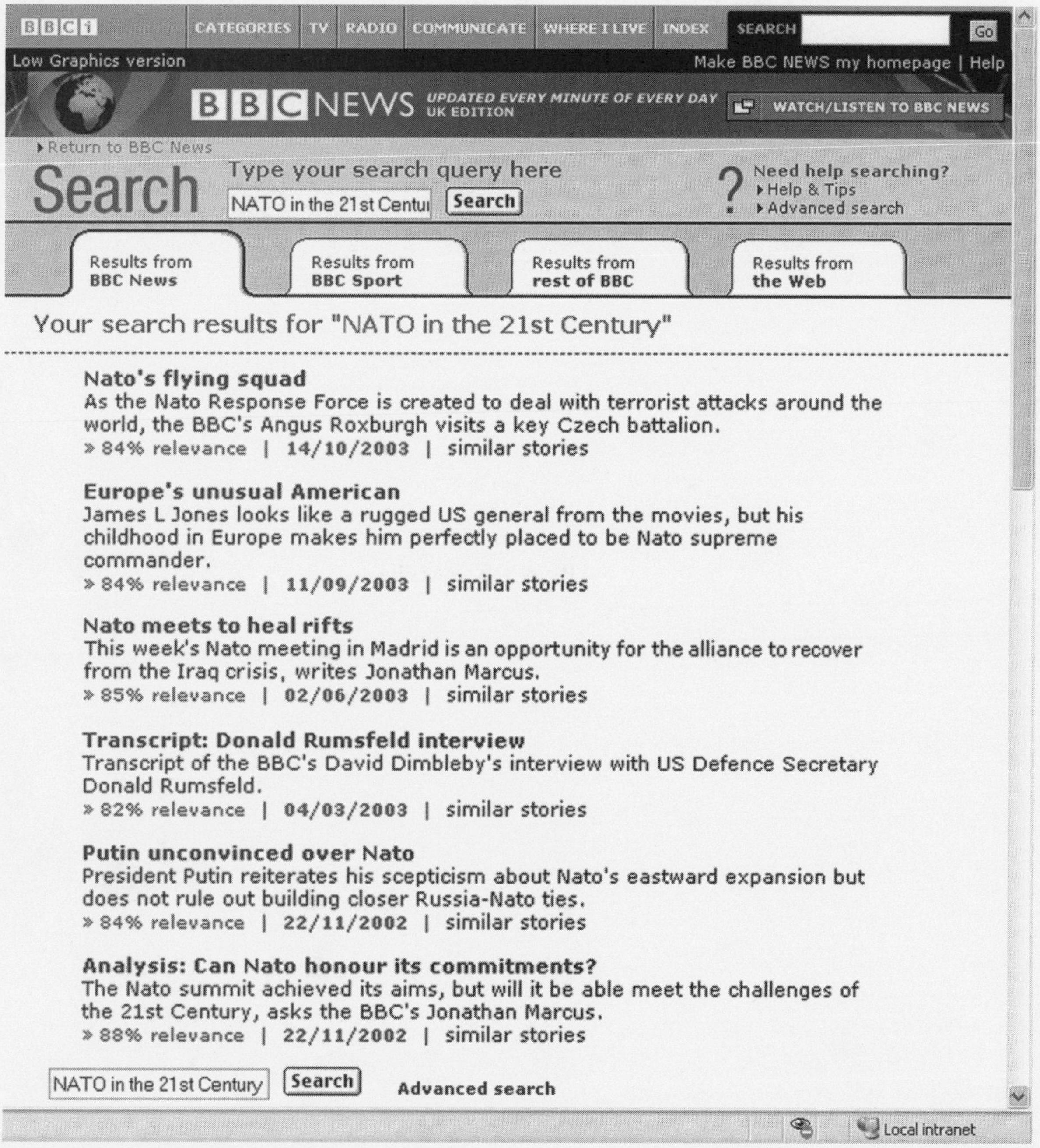
BBCi | CATEGORIES | TV | RADIO | COMMUNICATE | WHERE I LIVE | INDEX | SEARCH | Go

Low Graphics version — Make BBC NEWS my homepage | Help

BBC NEWS UPDATED EVERY MINUTE OF EVERY DAY UK EDITION — WATCH/LISTEN TO BBC NEWS

Return to BBC News

Search — Type your search query here: NATO in the 21st Centu — Search

Need help searching? Help & Tips, Advanced search

Results from BBC News | Results from BBC Sport | Results from rest of BBC | Results from the Web

Your search results for "NATO in the 21st Century"

Nato's flying squad
As the Nato Response Force is created to deal with terrorist attacks around the world, the BBC's Angus Roxburgh visits a key Czech battalion.
» 84% relevance | 14/10/2003 | similar stories

Europe's unusual American
James L Jones looks like a rugged US general from the movies, but his childhood in Europe makes him perfectly placed to be Nato supreme commander.
» 84% relevance | 11/09/2003 | similar stories

Nato meets to heal rifts
This week's Nato meeting in Madrid is an opportunity for the alliance to recover from the Iraq crisis, writes Jonathan Marcus.
» 85% relevance | 02/06/2003 | similar stories

Transcript: Donald Rumsfeld interview
Transcript of the BBC's David Dimbleby's interview with US Defence Secretary Donald Rumsfeld.
» 82% relevance | 04/03/2003 | similar stories

Putin unconvinced over Nato
President Putin reiterates his scepticism about Nato's eastward expansion but does not rule out building closer Russia-Nato ties.
» 84% relevance | 22/11/2002 | similar stories

Analysis: Can Nato honour its commitments?
The Nato summit achieved its aims, but will it be able meet the challenges of the 21st Century, asks the BBC's Jonathan Marcus.
» 88% relevance | 22/11/2002 | similar stories

NATO in the 21st Century — Search — Advanced search

Local intranet

Which result do you think would be the **most useful**? **Explain** your answer.

(Enquiry Skills, **2** marks)

[*END OF QUESTION PAPER*]

[BLANK PAGE]

2006 | General

[BLANK PAGE]

G

2640/402

NATIONAL QUALIFICATIONS 2006

MONDAY, 22 MAY
10.20 AM–11.50 AM

MODERN STUDIES
STANDARD GRADE
General Level

1 Read every question carefully.

2 Answer all questions as fully as you can.

3 If you cannot do a question, go on to the next one. Try again later.

4 In question 3, answer **one** section only; Section (A) The USA **or** Section (B) Russia **or** Section (C) China.

5 Write your answers in the answer book provided. Indicate clearly, in the left hand margin, the question and section of question being answered. Do not write in the right hand margin.

LI 2640/402 6/3/3/18770

SYLLABUS AREA 1—LIVING IN A DEMOCRACY

QUESTION 1

(*a*) *Trade union members have rights and responsibilities.*

Describe **one** right and **one** responsibility that a trade union member has.

(Knowledge & Understanding, **4** marks)

(*b*) Study Sources 1 and 2 below, then answer the question which follows.

SOURCE 1

Workers who are Trade Union Members (%)		
Year	***Male***	***Female***
1999	27·3	27·1
2001	26·6	27·1
2003	25·5	27·2

SOURCE 2

Trade Union Membership in Different Jobs (%)				
Type of Job	***1998***		***2002***	
	Males	***Females***	***Males***	***Females***
Managers and Administrators	18	21	16	22
Secretarial	30	22	31	23
Sales and Customer Services	18	12	13	13

Write down **two** conclusions about the membership of trade unions.

You must **only** use the information above.

You should write **one** conclusion about **each** of the following.

- Changes in male **or** female trade union membership between 1999 and 2003
- Changes in male **and** female trade union membership **in one of the jobs** between 1998 and 2002

(Enquiry Skills, **4** marks)

QUESTION 1 (CONTINUED)

(*c*) Study the information below, then answer the question which follows.

TRADE UNIONS AND THE SCOTTISH LABOUR PARTY

- Labour has the largest number of MSPs in the Scottish Parliament.
- A committee of the Labour Party in Scotland, which has trade union representatives on it, writes policies on which the Labour Party fights elections.
- Some trade unions give money to and campaign for Labour Party candidates in elections.
- Many MSPs who were elected at the 2003 election were not members of trade unions.
- A quarter of a million Scottish voters are members of trade unions.
- Trade unionists do not need to vote for the Labour Party in Scotland.

Trade unions play an important part in the election of Labour MSPs. Trade unions also play a part in policy making for the Labour Party.

View of Anne Hall

Give **two** reasons to **support** the view of Anne Hall.

(Enquiry Skills, **4** marks)

(*d*) *Local councillors and MSPs are representatives who work on behalf of people in their area.*

Choose **ONE** of the following representatives:

- local councillors
- MSPs.

Describe **two** ways in which *the representative you have chosen works on behalf of people in their area.*

(Knowledge & Understanding, **4** marks)

[Turn over

SYLLABUS AREA 2—CHANGING SOCIETY

QUESTION 2

(*a*) Many elderly people live in their own homes. Some of these homes have been adapted to meet their needs.

Give **two ways** in which homes can be adapted to meet the needs of some elderly people.

For **each** way, explain how it meets their needs.

(Knowledge & Understanding, **4** marks)

(*b*) Study Sources 1 and 2 below, then answer the question which follows.

SOURCE 1

Goodbye Geriatrics – Hello Geri-actives

Older people today have decided to become "Geri-actives" in their retirement. They want to enjoy new experiences. What these "Geri-actives" plan to do in retirement varies greatly. Their top six plans for "life after work" are gardening (60%), meeting friends (58%), travelling (57%), painting (14%), golf (11%) and writing novels (9%). Paying for these new activities may cost a lot of money. Arranging to have a good pension and saving as much as possible are essential for people nearing retirement.

SOURCE 2

The Percentage of Grandmothers who . . .

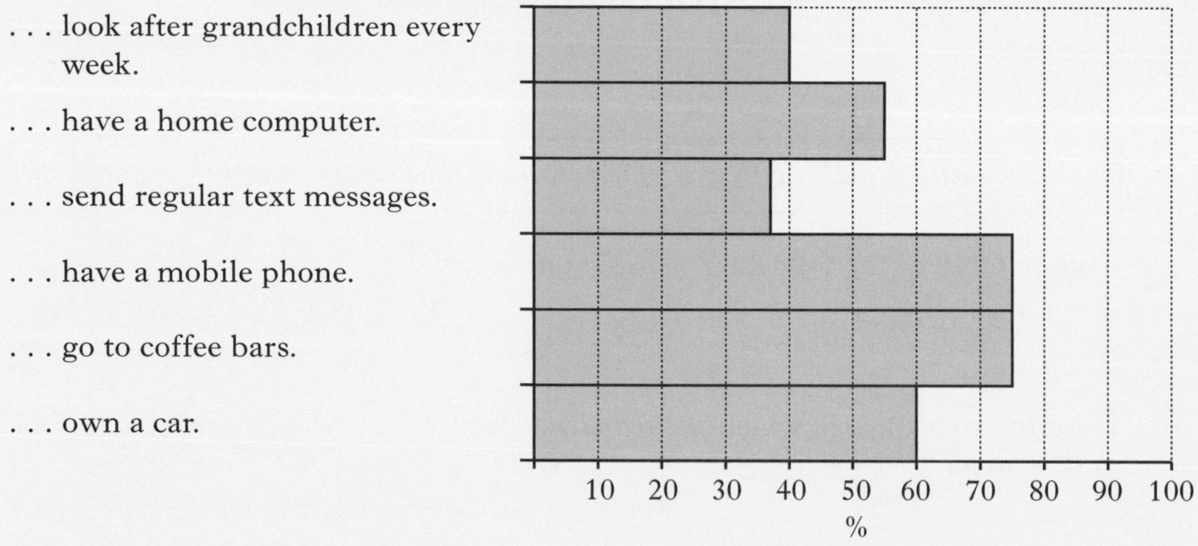

There are more elderly people today than ever before. Most grandmothers use very little technology. When most people retire, they just want to meet friends, travel and play golf. Elderly people should have a good pension.

View of Dennis Baxter

Using **only** Sources 1 and 2 above, write down **two** statements made by Dennis Baxter that are **exaggerated**.

Using the information in the Sources, give **one** reason why **each** of the statements you have chosen is **exaggerated**.

(Enquiry Skills, **4** marks)

QUESTION 2 (CONTINUED)

You are investigating the topic in the box below.

Local groups that help the elderly.

Answer questions (*c*), (*d*), (*e*) and (*f*) which follow.

(*c*) As part of the **Planning Stage**, give **two** relevant aims for your investigation.

(Enquiry Skills, **2** marks)

You decide to collect information about **local groups that help the elderly**.

(*d*) Give **two** relevant **ways** to gather information to help in your investigation.

(Enquiry Skills, **2** marks)

(*e*) For **one** of these ways, explain why it is a **good** way to get information to help in your investigation.

(Enquiry Skills, **2** marks)

You have been asked to develop your investigation. You decide to find out about a **national organisation** which helps the elderly.

You see the following advert in a newspaper.

Study the advert carefully, then answer the question which follows.

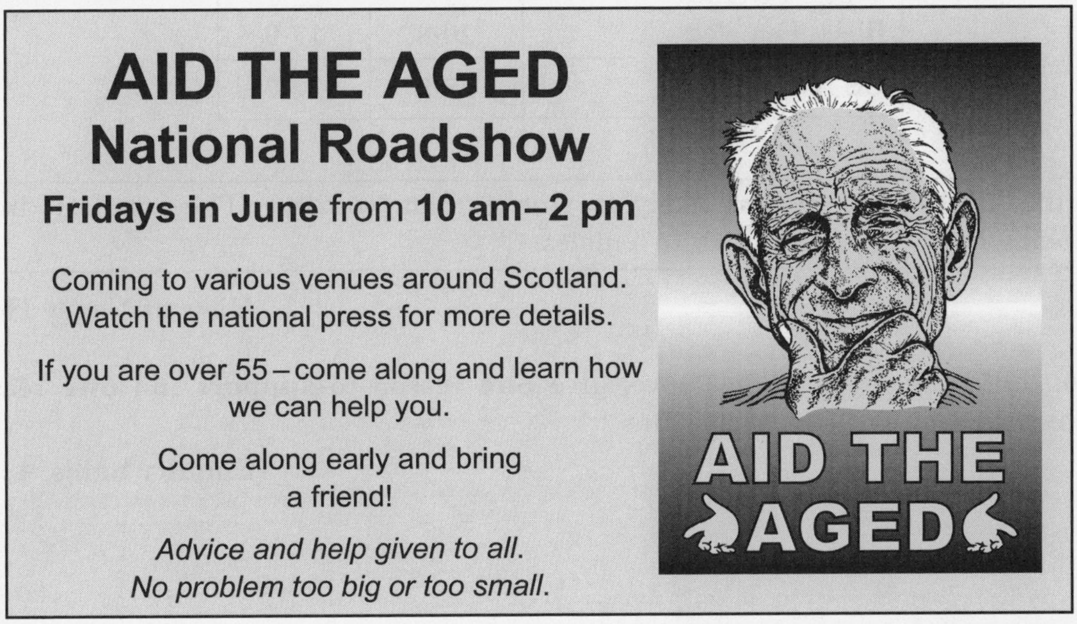

(*f*) You decide to visit the Aid The Aged National Roadshow to collect more information to help in your investigation.

Using **only** the information in the advert above, give **one difficulty** you might have in visiting this roadshow.

(Enquiry Skills, **2** marks)

SYLLABUS AREA 3—IDEOLOGIES

QUESTION 3

Answer **ONE** section only: Section (A)—The USA on pages *six* to *eight*

OR Section (B)—Russia on pages *nine* to *eleven*

OR Section (C)—China on pages *twelve* to *fourteen*

(A) **THE USA**

(*a*) *The American people can use the media to criticise the government.*

Describe **two** ways that *the American people can use the media to criticise the government.*

In your answer you **must** use American examples.

(Knowledge & Understanding, **4** marks)

(*b*) Study the information below, then answer the question which follows.

Cigarette Smoking amongst selected Groups in the USA (%)

	1990	**2001**
All Males	28·0	24·7
White Males	27·6	24·9
Black Males	32·8	27·6
All Females	22·9	20·8
White Females	23·5	22·1
Black Females	20·8	17·9
US Average	25·3	22·7

In the USA, men are less likely to smoke than women. The smallest drop in smoking has been amongst white females.

View of Nancy Holstein

Using **only** the information above, give **one** reason to **support** and **one** reason to **oppose** the view of Nancy Holstein.

(Enquiry Skills, **4** marks)

QUESTION 3 (A) (CONTINUED)

(*c*)

In recent years, many members of ethnic minority groups in the USA have seen an improvement in their standards of living.

Give **two** reasons to explain why *many members of ethnic minority groups in the USA have seen an improvement in their standards of living.*

In your answer you **must** use American examples.

(Knowledge & Understanding, **4** marks)

[Turn over

QUESTION 3 (A) (CONTINUED)

(*d*) Study the Timeline below, then answer the question which follows.

TIMELINE – WAR ON TERROR

KEY EVENTS 2001–2005

Date	Event
September 11 2001	Nearly 3000 people are killed when 2 airliners are hijacked by Al Qaeda terrorists and are crashed into the World Trade Centre in New York.
October 2001	American and allied troops invade Afghanistan to remove the Taliban government and destroy Al Qaeda forces in that country.
February 2003	Khalid Mohammed, a suspected terrorist and chief planner of the September 11 attacks, is captured in Pakistan.
March 2003	Thousands of US troops and their allies invade Iraq to remove the government of Saddam Hussein. He is accused of helping terrorist groups and of making weapons of mass destruction.
December 2003	Saddam Hussein is captured near Baghdad. It is expected that he will be charged with many crimes.
July 2005	Terrorist bombs explode on a bus and on a number of underground passenger trains in the city of London. Many people are killed and injured.

> Since September 11 2001, US troops have only invaded one country. In that time terrorists have killed more innocent people. America is the only country to suffer from terrorist attacks. Some important people have been captured in the war against terror.

Statements by an American Journalist

Using **only** the information above, write down **two** statements made by the American Journalist which are **exaggerated**.

Using the Timeline, give **one** reason why **each** of the statements you have chosen is **exaggerated**.

(Enquiry Skills, **4** marks)

NOW GO TO QUESTION 4 ON PAGE FIFTEEN

QUESTION 3 (CONTINUED)

(B) **RUSSIA**

(*a*) *The Russian people can use the media to criticise the government.*

Describe **two** ways that *the Russian people can use the media to criticise the government.*

In your answer you **must** use Russian examples.

(Knowledge & Understanding, **4** marks)

(*b*) Study the information below, then answer the question which follows.

Salaries of People in selected Occupations in Russia

Average Salary (US Dollars)			
Occupation	***2002***	***2003***	***% Change***
Financial Controller	500	650	+30
IT Company Director	3000	4500	+50
Lawyer	1750	2100	+20
Personnel Director	1250	2000	+60
Sales Manager	400	900	+125
Secretary	300	325	+8
Training Manager	750	1050	+40

Jobs in IT and the Law have the highest salaries. These jobs have also seen the biggest change in salaries between 2002 and 2003.

View of Natalia Medvedev

Using **only** the information above, give **one** reason to **support** and **one** reason to **oppose** the view of Natalia Medvedev.

(Enquiry Skills, **4** marks)

[Turn over

QUESTION 3 (B) (CONTINUED)

(*c*)

People living in the major cities tend to have a better standard of living than those living in other parts of Russia.

Give **two** reasons why *people living in the major cities tend to have a better standard of living than those living in other parts of Russia.*

In your answer you **must** use Russian examples.

(Knowledge & Understanding, **4** marks)

QUESTION 3 (B) (CONTINUED)

(*d*) Study the Timeline below, then answer the question which follows.

TIMELINE – CHECHNYA

KEY EVENTS 2000–2004

Date	Event
May 2000	President Putin of Russia declares that Chechnya will be ruled directly from Moscow. He is determined to defeat the Chechen rebels by all means available to him.
November 2001	Official talks take place between Russian authorities and Chechen rebels on a possible peace settlement. Talks break up without agreement.
December 2001	A captured rebel Chechen army commander is sentenced to life imprisonment by a court in Moscow.
October 2002	Chechen rebels seize a theatre in Moscow, the Russian capital, and hold 800 people hostage. 120 hostages are killed by the rebels when Russian forces storm the building. Most of the rebels are then killed by the Russian troops in the battle which follows.
March 2003	Russian people are pleased with the result of the ballot in Chechnya which shows a majority of Chechens in favour of remaining part of Russia.
May 2004	Recently elected President of Chechnya, Akhmad Kadyrov, killed in a bomb blast carried out by Chechen rebels.

It is the Chechen rebels who have carried out all the killings. Elections have taken place in Chechnya. Important politicians on both sides have been directly involved in the war. A settlement between the two sides is within reach.

Statements by a Russian Journalist

Using **only** the information above, write down **two** statements made by the Russian Journalist, which are **exaggerated**.

Using the Timeline, give **one** reason why **each** of the statements you have chosen is **exaggerated**.

(Enquiry Skills, **4** marks)

NOW GO TO QUESTION 4 ON PAGE FIFTEEN

QUESTION 3 (CONTINUED)

(C) **CHINA**

(*a*) *The Chinese people are not allowed to criticise the government.*

Describe **two** actions which the Chinese Government might take to deal with those who do criticise the government.

In your answer you **must** use Chinese examples.

(Knowledge & Understanding, **4** marks)

(*b*) Study the information below, then answer the question which follows.

Population with Internet Access in selected Countries (%)

Country	*2003*	*2004*	*2005*
China	8	10	25
USA	43	47	54
Russia	15	17	24
Japan	48	51	53
UK	40	42	46

China has always had the lowest Internet access of all the world's major countries. However, it is showing the fastest growth.

View of Li Tie

Using **only** the information above, give **one** reason to **support** and **one** reason to **oppose** the view of Li Tie.

(Enquiry Skills, **4** marks)

QUESTION 3 (C) (CONTINUED)

(*c*)

People living in the major cities tend to have a better standard of living than those living in other parts of China.

Give **two** reasons why *people living in the major cities tend to have a better standard of living than those living in other parts of China.*

In your answer you **must** use Chinese examples.

(Knowledge & Understanding, **4** marks)

[Turn over

QUESTION 3 (C) (CONTINUED)

(*d*) Study the Timeline below, then answer the question which follows.

TIMELINE–THE THREE GORGES DAM PROJECT

KEY EVENTS 1992–2009

Date	Event
1992	Work starts on the dam. The project is expected to take 17 years to complete and will open in 2009.
February 1993	20 000 people start work around the clock on the dam. 250 000 people will have had jobs building the dam by the time it is finished.
July 1993	Journalist Dai Qing is jailed for ten months for criticising the project. Over the next year, hundreds of others are also jailed by the Chinese government.
1999	The government begins an inquiry into safety at the site after 40 workers are killed in an accident.
2003	The Chinese government claims that only 1·2 million people will lose their homes when the valley is flooded. Some people claim it will be 2 million.
2009	Over 100 million people will have electricity for the first time when the dam is finished.

The Three Gorges Dam is a huge building project. Every Chinese person will benefit when the project is finished. Electricity will improve the lives of many Chinese people. Everyone in China supports the project.

Statements by a Chinese Journalist

Using **only** the information above, write down **two** statements made by the Chinese Journalist which are **exaggerated**.

Using the Timeline, give **one** reason why **each** of the statements you have chosen is **exaggerated**.

(Enquiry Skills, **4** marks)

NOW GO TO QUESTION 4 ON PAGE FIFTEEN

SYLLABUS AREA 4—INTERNATIONAL RELATIONS

QUESTION 4

(*a*) **United Nations Specialised Agencies**

FAO — Food and Agricultural Organisation

unicef — United Nations Children's Fund

WHO — World Health Organisation

Choose **one** of the UN Specialised Agencies above.

Describe **two** ways in which the agency you have chosen tries to meet the **needs** of people in Africa.

(Knowledge & Understanding, **4** marks)

(*b*) Study Sources 1 and 2 below, then answer the question which follows.

SOURCE 1

United Nations Press Release

A large number of people have been forced to leave their homes and over 50 000 have been killed in the Darfur region of Sudan since 2003. Darfur itself is a very dry area in the west of Sudan, the largest country in Africa.

There has been conflict between black Africans and Arabs in the region for many years. Due to this there is a lack of aid and children are now dying of hunger.

SOURCE 2

Sudanese Government Press Release

Darfur is a desert area in the west of the largest country in Africa, Sudan. It is well known that there is fighting between the Arabs and black Africans in Darfur which has caused many deaths.

Our country needs more money to be able to develop. However, everybody has enough to eat. A large number of people have chosen to leave their homes in Darfur and move to other countries such as Chad.

Sources 1 and 2 give different views about **what has been happening in the Darfur region of Sudan**.

Write down **two** differences between these views.

You **must** only use information from the Sources above.

(Enquiry Skills, **4** marks)

[Turn over for Questions 4(*c*) and 4(*d*) on *Page sixteen*

QUESTION 4 (CONTINUED)

(*c*)

TIED AID – SOME FACTS

- Tied aid cuts the value of aid by 25–40%.
- The United Kingdom is one of only four countries stopping tied aid.
- 60–75% of Canadian aid is tied.
- The USA, Germany, Japan and France still insist on most of their aid being "tied".
- The USA makes sure that 80c in every dollar is returned to the USA.
- The USA insists that anti-AIDS drugs are bought from the USA instead of cheaper products from South Africa, India or Brazil.

Give **two** reasons why some rich countries give tied aid to countries in Africa.

(Knowledge & Understanding, **4** marks)

(*d*) Study the information below, then answer the question which follows.

Selected Statistics for three African Countries in 2004

	Benin 	Kenya 	Nigeria 
Infant deaths (per 1000 live births)	85	62	70
Life expectancy (years)	51	45	50
HIV/AIDS in adult population (%)	1·9	6·7	5·4
Population below poverty line (%)	37	50	60
Literacy rate (%)	41	85	68
Voting age (years)	18	18	18

Statements made by Alison Grey, Aid Worker

- Benin has a smaller percentage of its population living in poverty than either Kenya or Nigeria.
- Nigeria has the highest rate of HIV/AIDS amongst adults.
- Infant deaths are lowest in Benin.
- The literacy rate in all three countries is very similar.
- Life expectancy is lowest in Kenya.

Using **only** the information above, write down **two** statements made by Alison Grey which are **correct**.

Using the information, give **one** reason why **each** of the statements you have chosen is **correct**.

(Enquiry Skills, **4** marks)

[*END OF QUESTION PAPER*]

2006 | Credit

[BLANK PAGE]

C

2640/403

NATIONAL QUALIFICATIONS 2006

MONDAY, 22 MAY
1.00 PM – 3.00 PM

MODERN STUDIES
STANDARD GRADE
Credit Level

1 Read every question carefully.

2 Answer all questions as fully as you can.

3 If you cannot do a question, go on to the next one. Try again later.

4 In question 3, answer **one** section only: Section (A) The USA **or** Section (B) Russia **or** Section (C) China.

5 Write your answers in the answer book provided. Indicate clearly, in the left hand margin, the question and section of question being answered. Do not write in the right hand margin.

LI 2640/403 6/14270

SYLLABUS AREA 1—LIVING IN A DEMOCRACY

QUESTION 1

(*a*) *Candidates rely on help from party workers and volunteers during election campaigns.*

Describe, **in detail**, the ways in which party workers and volunteers can help during election campaigns.

(Knowledge & Understanding, **6** marks)

(*b*) *In a democracy, it is important that people use their right to vote.*

Explain, **in detail,** why it is important for people to use their **right** to vote.

(Knowledge & Understanding, **4** marks)

You have been asked to carry out **two** investigations.

The first investigation is on the topic in the box below.

Voting systems used in elections in Scotland.

Now answer questions (*c*) and (*d*) which follow.

(*c*) State a relevant **hypothesis** for your investigation.

(Enquiry Skills, **2** marks)

(*d*) Give **two** relevant **aims** to help you prove or disprove your hypothesis.

(Enquiry Skills, **2** marks)

QUESTION 1 (CONTINUED)

The second investigation is on the topic in the box below.

Peoples' attitude towards voting.

Now answer questions (*e*) and (*f*) which follow.

(*e*) While collecting information for your investigation, you find the following survey result.

Question: Can people influence political decisions by voting?	
Age	**% saying yes**
16–19	17
20–29	26
30–39	25
40–49	27
50–64	25
65+	22
Source: Home Office Citizenship Survey: (Statistics Directorate), September 2004 [based on 9600 replies, UK wide]	

Give **two** detailed reasons why the above survey is a **good** source of information to use in your investigation.

(Enquiry Skills, **4** marks)

(*f*) You then decide to collect more information by carrying out your own survey about peoples' attitude to voting in your local area.

Give **one other relevant** question which you could include in your survey.

(Enquiry Skills, **2** marks)

[Turn over

SYLLABUS AREA 2—CHANGING SOCIETY

QUESTION 2

(*a*) **Recent Government Policies to improve Employment Opportunities**

new deal

Skillseekers

jobcentreplus

ema
Education Maintenance Allowance

MODERN
APPRENTICESHIPS

Choose **two** policies from the list above.

Describe, **in detail**, the ways in which each policy has tried to improve employment opportunities.

(Knowledge & Understanding, **6** marks)

QUESTION 2 (CONTINUED)

(*b*) Study Sources 1 and 2 below, then answer the question which follows.

SOURCE 1

Households by type in Scotland, 1981–2003 (%)			
	1981	**1991**	**2003**
Single Adult	7·2	12·9	15·9
Pensioner (single or couple)	28·9	29·8	30·8
Couple no children	28·4	27·1	26·7
Single Parent with children	2·3	4·9	5·8
Couple with children	33·2	25·3	20·8

SOURCE 2

Selected Scottish households living in poverty (%)

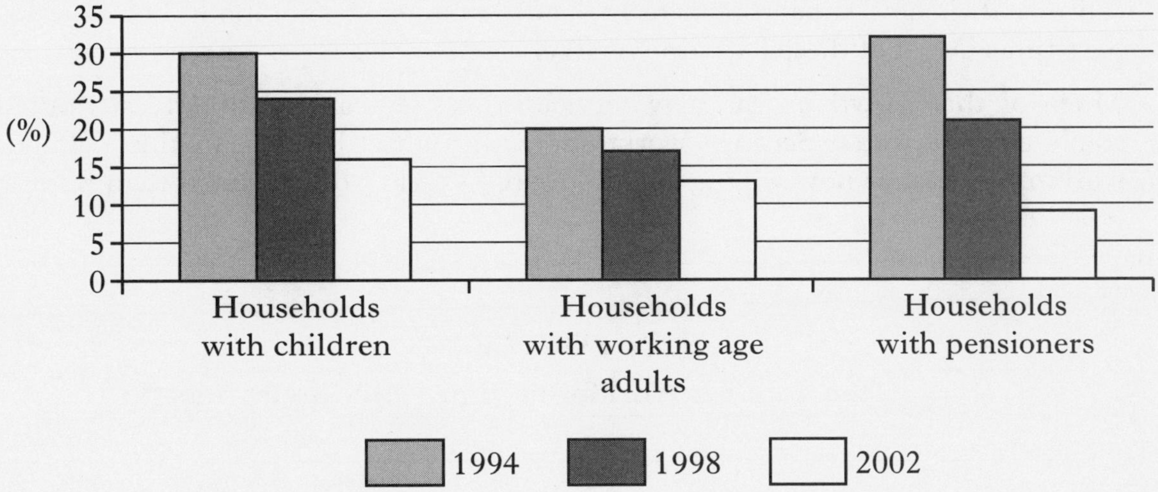

> Households consisting of pensioners have grown the most in percentage terms. However, they have experienced less of an improvement in the quality of their lives than other groups.

View of Sandy Mathieson

Give **two** reasons to **oppose** the view of Sandy Mathieson.

(Enquiry Skills, **4** marks)

[Turn over

QUESTION 2 (CONTINUED)

(*c*) Study Sources 1, 2, 3 and 4 below and opposite, then answer the question which follows.

SOURCE 1

Scotland – a country in industrial change

The traditional male dominated production and construction industries in Scotland are all in decline. In 2000, Scotland only had 35 000 working in oil, gas and fishing, traditionally some of Scotland's key industries. The new growth industries in Scotland are all service industries such as call centres, Biotechnology, Software and e-Business.

A new service industry which has grown in Scotland is call centres. In 1998, Scotland's call centre industry employed 16 000 workers, of which 42% were women. By 2000, this figure had grown to 37 000. Five years on, there are 60 000 people employed in them. Considerable growth is predicted in the industry and of the 290 call centres, 92 predict increased employment by 2007. Around 67% of Scottish call centre staff is now female. 75% of the staff is under 35 and about 33% of the staff is part-time. Most of these part-time workers are female.

Much of this growth in the new service industries can be directly attributed to a stable and motivated Scottish workforce with highly developed skills. It is also a workforce which is now willing to have more flexible work patterns than traditionally was the case.

SOURCE 2

The Scottish Workforce (figures in thousands)				
	Males		Females	
	1998	2002	1998	2002
Agriculture, Forestry and Fishing	31	29	8	8
Production and Construction Industries				
Construction	113	108	24	14
Energy and Water	37	32	9	9
Manufacturing	227	189	99	74
Service Industries				
Banking, Finance and Insurance	156	187	170	191
Distribution, Hotels and Catering, Repairs	214	238	289	308
Public Administration, Education and Health	163	176	394	458
Transport and Communication	86	93	28	32
Other Services	52	62	54	63
Total employed	**1079**	**1114**	**1075**	**1157**

QUESTION 2(*c*) (CONTINUED)

SOURCE 3

Working conditions – Number of part-time workers in Scotland (000s)

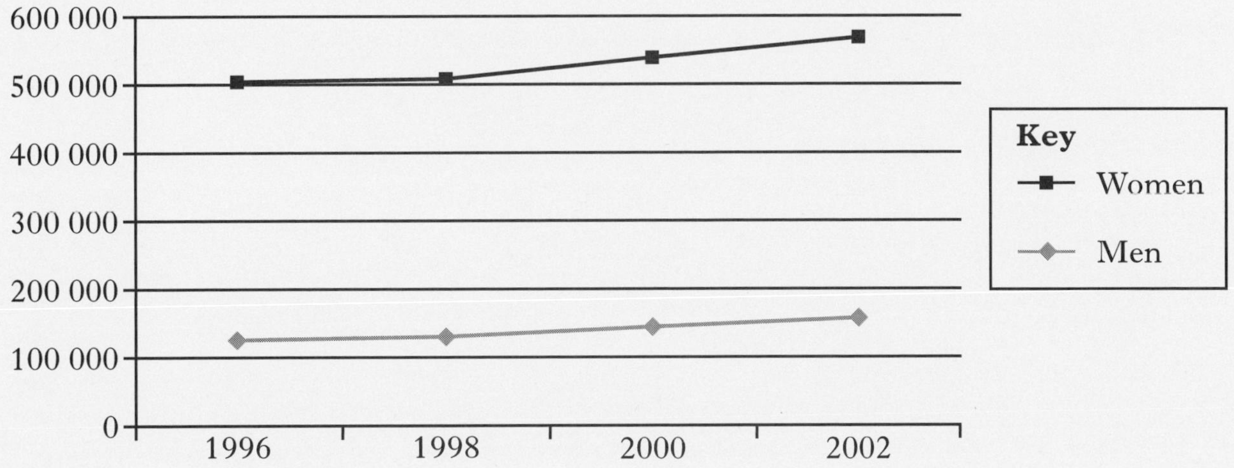

SOURCE 4

Working conditions – Female earnings as a percentage (%) of male earnings

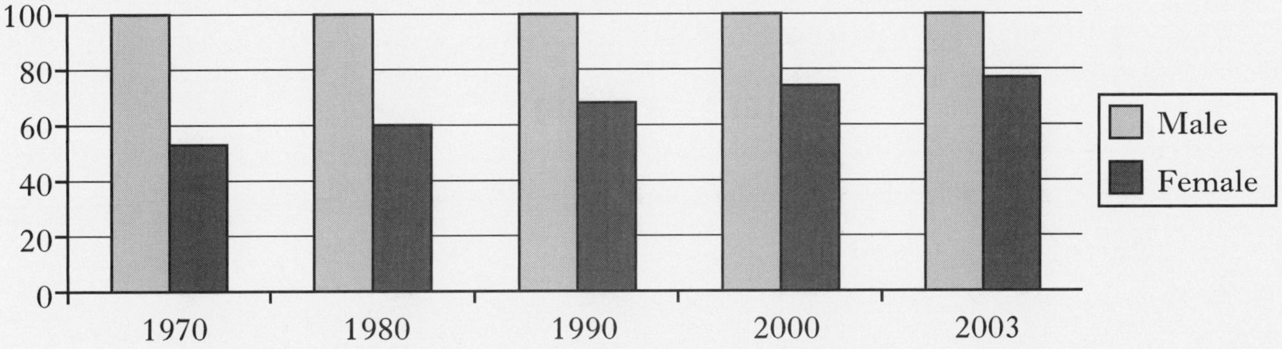

Women are becoming more important to the Scottish economy in the 21st century. Furthermore, this is reflected in the changes in their pay and conditions.

View of Tom Anderson

Using **only** Sources 1, 2, 3 and 4, explain **the extent to which** Tom Anderson could be accused of being **selective in the use of facts**.

(Enquiry Skills, **8** marks)

[Turn over

[BLANK PAGE]

SYLLABUS AREA 3—IDEOLOGIES

QUESTION 3

Answer **one** section only:		Section (A)—The USA on pages *nine* to *eleven*
	OR	Section (B)—Russia on pages *thirteen* to *fifteen*
	OR	Section (C)—China on pages *seventeen* to *nineteen*

(A) **THE USA**

(*a*) *In the USA, citizens have both political rights and the responsibilities that go with them.*

Describe, **in detail**, the ***political rights*** *of American citizens and the* ***responsibilities*** *that go with them.*

In your answer you **must** use American examples.

(Knowledge and Understanding, **8** marks)

[Turn over

QUESTION 3 (A) (CONTINUED)

(*b*) Study Sources 1, 2, 3 and 4 and the information on New York City, then answer the question which follows.

Information about New York City

Population of the 5 New York Boroughs

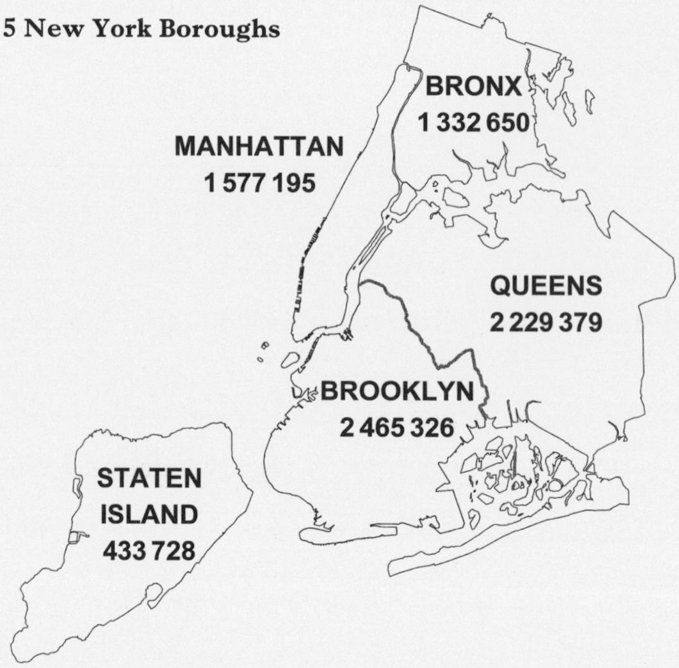

New York has a population of 8 008 278, which makes it America's largest city.
It has experienced a 10% increase in its population since 1990.
It is a city with a great mix of different races, nationalities and cultures.
The city is itself divided into five Boroughs: The Bronx, Brooklyn, Manhattan, Queens and Staten Island.

Racial Composition of Population in New York City		
White	2 801 267	35·0%
Hispanic	2 160 554	27·0%
Black	1 962 154	24·5%
Asian/Pacific Islanders	783 058	9·8%
Native Americans	17 321	0·2%
Other	283 924	3·5%

SOURCE 1

New York Boroughs: Population in 2000 by Race (%)

	Bronx	Brooklyn	Manhattan	Queens	Staten Island
White	14·5	34·6	45·8	32·9	71·3
Hispanic	48·4	19·8	27·2	25·0	12·1
Black	31·2	34·4	15·3	19·0	8·9
Asian/Pacific Islanders	2·9	7·5	9·4	17·5	5·6
Native Americans	0·3	0·2	0·2	0·3	0·1
Others	2·7	3·5	2·1	5·3	2·0

QUESTION 3 (A) (*b*) (CONTINUED)

SOURCE 2

New York Boroughs: Educational Attainment in 2000 by those aged 25+ (%)

	Did not complete High School	College Graduate
Bronx	38	15
Brooklyn	31	22
Manhattan	21	49
Queens	26	24
Staten Island	17	23

SOURCE 3

New York Boroughs: Crime Rate in 2000 (per 100 000 people)

	Person Crime	Property Crime	Total
Bronx	1112	2369	3481
Brooklyn	1024	2134	3158
Manhattan	895	3822	4717
Queens	583	2079	2662
Staten Island	332	1400	1732

SOURCE 4

New York Boroughs: Family Finances and Poverty Statistics in 2000

	Average Household Income ($)	Families in Poverty (%)
Bronx	28 000	27
Brooklyn	32 000	22
Manhattan	48 000	18
Queens	42 000	12
Staten Island	55 000	8

Using **only** the information about New York City and Sources 1, 2, 3, 4 above and opposite, what **conclusions** can be drawn about the ways in which the Boroughs are different from each other, and from the city as a whole?

You must **make** and **justify** a conclusion about **each** of the following headings.

- The Borough whose racial composition is **least** like that of the city as a whole
- The relationship between person crime rates and educational attainment
- The relationship between race and family finances
- The desirability of Manhattan as a Borough to live in

(Enquiry Skills, **8** marks)

[NOW GO TO QUESTION 4 ON PAGE 21]

[BLANK PAGE]

QUESTION 3 (CONTINUED)

(B) **RUSSIA**

(*a*) | *In Russia, citizens have both political rights and the responsibilities that go with them.* |

Describe, **in detail**, the ***political rights*** *of Russian citizens and the* ***responsibilities*** *that go with them.*

In your answer, you **must** use Russian examples.

(Knowledge and Understanding, **8** marks)

[Turn over

QUESTION 3 (B) (CONTINUED)

(*b*) Study Sources 1, 2, 3 and 4 and the information on Russia, then answer the question which follows.

Information about Russia

Russia is the biggest country in Asia with a total population of 144 million and a labour force of 72 million. It has large deposits of coal, natural gas, oil and many other valuable minerals. Russia is one of the major economic powers in the world. Its economy has grown fast since the end of Communist rule in 1991. It earns billions of dollars from oil and petrol exports and has a total GDP of $1282 billion. Russia relies on trade with several neighbouring countries and it sells over 16% of its exports to, and buys 19% of its imports from, just five of its neighbours.

Urban/Rural Divide

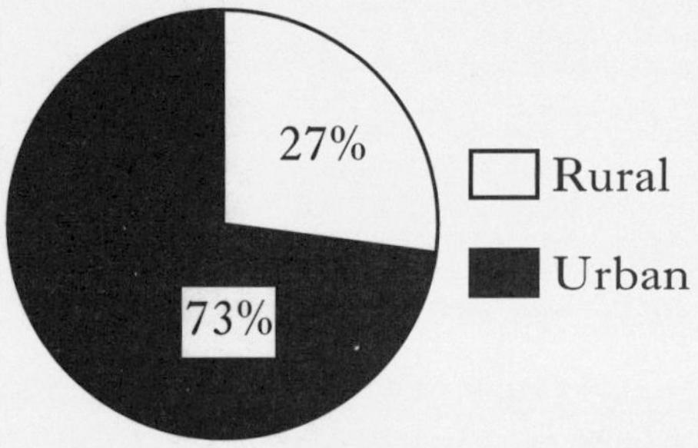

Russia and its neighbours

Economic Information		
Sector	**Employment (%)**	**Contribution to Wealth of Country (%)**
Agriculture	12	5
Industry	24	35
Services	64	60

SOURCE 1

Selected Countries: Trade with Russia (%)

	Imports from Russia	Exports to Russia
Japan	1·7	3·1
Mongolia	33·9	6·5
Kazakhstan	34·9	15·5
Norway	2·4	2·5
North Korea	2·1	8·1

QUESTION 3 (B) (*b*) (CONTINUED)

SOURCE 2

Urban/Rural Divide in some of Russia's neighbours (%)

	Urban	Rural
Japan	79	21
Mongolia	57	43
Kazakhstan	56	44
Norway	75	25
North Korea	61	39

SOURCE 3

Employment in different sectors of the economy for some of Russia's neighbours (%)

	Agriculture	Industry	Services
Japan	5	25	70
Mongolia	79	6	15
Kazakhstan	20	30	50
Norway	4	22	74
North Korea	36	48	16

SOURCE 4

Contribution of each sector to the GDP for some of Russia's neighbours (%)

	Agriculture	Industry	Services
Japan	1	26	73
Mongolia	20	21	59
Kazakhstan	8	37	55
Norway	2	36	62
North Korea	30	34	36

Using **only** the information on Russia and Sources 1, 2, 3, 4 above and opposite, what **conclusions** can be drawn about the relationship between **Russia and her neighbours**?

You must **make** and **justify** a conclusion about **each** of the following headings.

- The urban/rural divide in Russia compared with some of her neighbours
- The relationship between the urban/rural divide and employment in agriculture
- The relationship between employment in services and their contribution to GDP
- The importance of Russia to the economies of the neighbouring countries

(Enquiry Skills, **8** marks)

[NOW GO TO QUESTION 4 ON PAGE 21]

[BLANK PAGE]

QUESTION 3 (CONTINUED)

(C) **CHINA**

(*a*)

The Communist government in China gives citizens certain rights. In return, citizens are expected to accept their responsibilities.

Describe, **in detail**, the ***rights*** *that Chinese citizens have and the* ***responsibilities*** *that go with them.*

In your answer, you **must** use Chinese examples.

(Knowledge and Understanding, **8** marks)

[Turn over

QUESTION 3 (C) (CONTINUED)

(*b*) Study Sources 1, 2, 3 and 4 and the information on China, then answer the question which follows.

Information about China

China is the second biggest country in Asia with a total population of 1·3 billion and a labour force of 744 million. It has large deposits of coal, natural gas, oil and many other valuable minerals. The government in China has turned the country into the major economic power in the region with the fastest growing economy in the world. China relies on trade with several countries in the region and has a total GDP of $6449 billion. It sells almost 21% of its exports to, and buys 25% of its imports from, just five of its neighbours.

Urban/Rural Divide

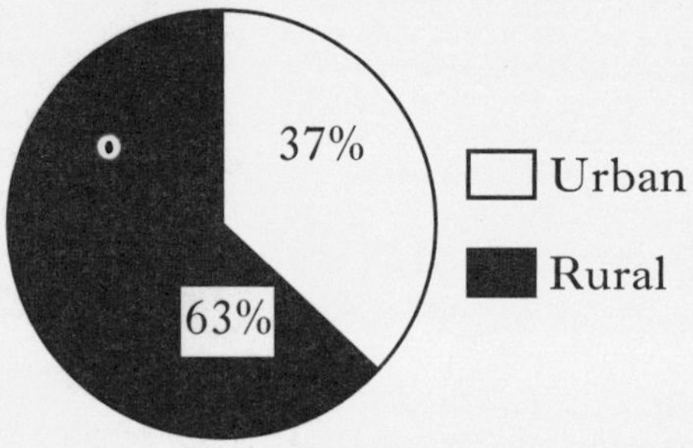

China and its neighbours

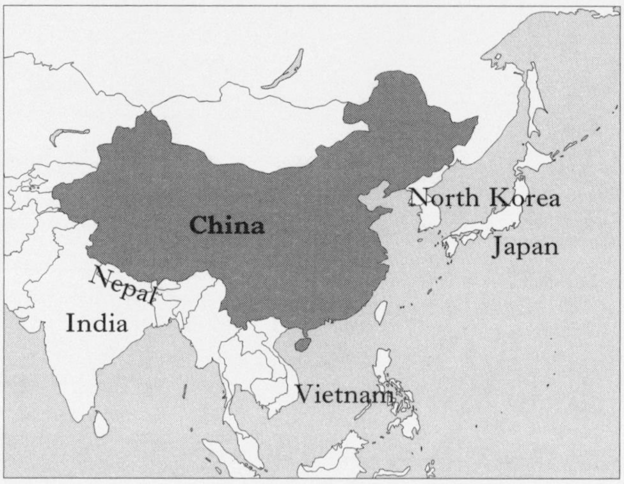

Economic Information		
Sector	**Employment (%)**	**Contribution to wealth of country (%)**
Agriculture	50	15
Industry	22	53
Services	28	32

SOURCE 1

Selected Countries: Trade with China (%)

	Imports from China	Exports to China
Japan	19·7	12·1
India	4·5	6·3
Vietnam	13·6	6·2
Nepal	13·5	0·5
North Korea	39·7	28·4

QUESTION 3 (C) (*b*) (CONTINUED)

SOURCE 2

Urban/Rural Divide in some of China's neighbours (%)

	Urban	**Rural**
Japan	79	21
India	28	72
Vietnam	25	75
Nepal	12	88
North Korea	61	39

SOURCE 3

Employment in different sectors of the economy for some of China's neighbours (%)

	Agriculture	**Industry**	**Services**
Japan	5	25	70
India	60	17	23
Vietnam	63	23	14
Nepal	81	3	16
North Korea	36	48	16

SOURCE 4

Contribution of each sector to the GDP for some of China's neighbours (%)

	Agriculture	**Industry**	**Services**
Japan	1	26	73
India	24	28	48
Vietnam	22	40	38
Nepal	40	20	40
North Korea	30	34	36

Using **only** the information on China and Sources 1, 2, 3, 4 above and opposite, what **conclusions** can be drawn about the relationship between **China and her neighbours**?

You must **make** and **justify** a conclusion about **each** of the following headings.

- The urban/rural divide in China compared with some of her neighbours
- The relationship between the urban/rural divide and employment in agriculture
- The relationship between employment in services and their contribution to GDP
- The importance of China to the economies of the neighbouring countries

(Enquiry Skills, **8** marks)

[NOW GO TO QUESTION 4 ON PAGE 21]

[BLANK PAGE]

SYLLABUS AREA 4—INTERNATIONAL RELATIONS

QUESTION 4

(*a*) *In recent years some European countries and their allies have expanded their military actions beyond Europe.*

Explain, **in detail**, the reasons why *some European countries and their allies have expanded their military actions beyond Europe*.

In answering this question, you must refer to:

- A description of some of these actions.
- The reasons why such actions were taken.

Your answer **must** refer to recent examples you have studied.

(Knowledge & Understanding, **8** marks)

[Turn over

QUESTION 4 (CONTINUED)

(*b*) Study Sources 1, 2, 3 and 4 below and opposite, then answer the question which follows.

THE GREAT EUROPEAN DEBATE

SOURCE 1

Membership of the European Union (EU)

1958 Belgium, France, W Germany, Luxembourg, Italy and the Netherlands
1973 Denmark, Ireland and the UK
1981 Greece
1986 Portugal and Spain
1995 Austria, Finland and Sweden
2004 Cyprus, the Czech Republic, Estonia, Hungary, Latvia, Lithuania, Malta, Poland, Slovakia and Slovenia.

For the future, Bulgaria, Croatia, Romania and Turkey still wish to join the EU.

Opinion Poll carried out in selected countries
Question: If the EU were scrapped, how would you feel?

	Unhappy (%)	Delighted (%)	Don't care (%)	Don't know (%)
Belgium	29	7	53	11
Finland	22	28	41	9
Germany	30	14	40	16
Ireland	44	3	34	19
UK	16	27	45	12
EU average	28	14	45	13

The 2004 elections for the European Parliament highlighted many issues of importance to the people of Europe. Just over 44% of the 350 million eligible voters in 25 member states cast their ballots, making this one of the biggest democratic exercises in the world.

Many pro-Europeans had great hopes for the new member countries in these elections but only 20% of the electorate in Poland voted, despite the huge amount of EU funding the country is likely to receive over the next few years. The Poles, along with the majority of EU voters, rejected the party in government, using this as a protest vote about domestic issues.

SOURCE 2: Percentage of votes gained by selected parties in UK elections for the European Parliament (1999 and 2004)

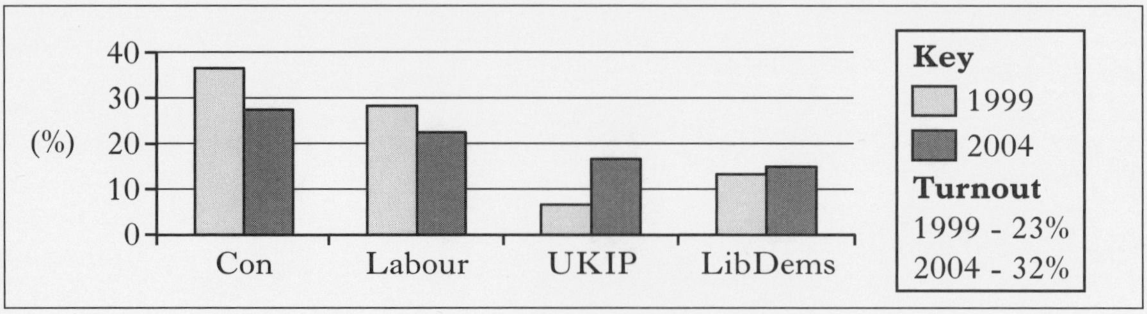

QUESTION 4 (*b*) (CONTINUED)

SOURCE 3: Attitude of selected political parties towards the European Union

SOURCE 4: Results of an Opinion Poll

Question: If there were a referendum on whether Britain should stay in or get out of the EU, how would you vote?

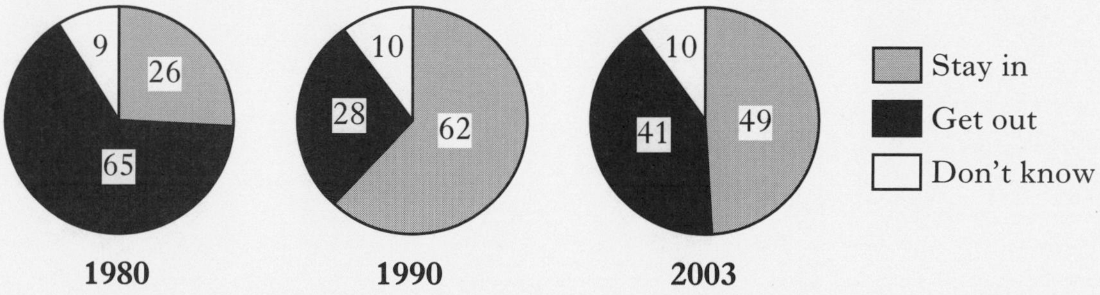

People in Britain and in other European countries no longer wish to be part of the European Union.

View of a UKIP voter

Using **only** sources 1, 2, 3 and 4 above and opposite, provide evidence **for** and **against** the view of the UKIP voter.

Overall, do you think the evidence **supports** the view? Give a reason for your answer.

(Enquiry Skills, **10** marks)

[*END OF QUESTION PAPER*]

[BLANK PAGE]

[BLANK PAGE]

[BLANK PAGE]

[BLANK PAGE]

Acknowledgements

Leckie & Leckie is grateful to the copyright holders, as credited, for permission to use their material.
The following companies/individuals have very generously given permission to reproduce their copyright material free of charge:

Her Majesty's Stationery Office for an extract from *Scottish Community Care Statistics* (2002 Credit paper p 8);
Shelter for use of their logo (2003 General p 2);
Greenpeace for use of their logo (2003 General p 2);
OECD for the table 'Social Statistics – Russia' adapted from *OECD* (2003 General paper p 8);
The Economist for the extract 'Factfile on European Involvement', 22 September, 2001 (2003 General paper p 13);
The United Nations for an extract from their website (2003 Credit p 21);
Unicef for their logo (2004 General paper p 13 and 2006 General p 15);
Who for their logo (2004 General paper p 13);
ICM Research for the table 'Support for Selected Political Parties in Opinion Polls' (2004 General paper p 3);
Scottish Enterprise National for the logos for Skillseekers and Modern Apprenticeships (2006 Credit p 4);
The Labour Party for use of their logo (2006 Credit paper p 23).